*I have witnessed Terry's marriage and read his book. This man
knows how to make a marriage work. Even after 45 years of
marriage I benefited from Terry's insights and pure common sense.
Want to make your marriage extraordinary? Read this!!*

Gordon D. Wusyk, B.Ed., CFP, CLU, CH.F.C., TEP
Predictable Futures Inc.
The Business Family Centre
Edmonton, Alberta
Married 45 years

*It was fabulous. Lots of guys were given license to change their lives by
[Terry's] seminar. Great work!! ... Many Blessings to you and Laura
... your transparency as a couple is a gift to couples all over Canada.*

Thanks again.

Don Crompton
National Director, Young Life Canada
Langley, British Columbia
Married 39 years

*Terry Bachynski understands that love isn't something that 'happens' to
us, something over which we have no control. Love is a choice we make, a
verb we act out, a commitment we live by. In this book he communicates
this vital truth to men, using primarily stories - sometimes light-hearted,
sometimes more poignant and gut-wrenching - of his own mistakes and
hard-won learning experiences. I've been married for nearly thirty years,
and this book rings true for me on almost every page. I highly recommend it.*

Tim Chesterton
Pastor, St. Margaret's Anglican Church
Edmonton, Alberta
Married 30 years

It was a "God-incidence" that led me to read Terry's book, and I believe that it was His way to reach me and help me to address some of the unresolved issues I still struggled with - even after 31 years of married life.

Through reading about this couple's heart-wrenching adversity and onward to their significant successes, I discovered what was weak or missing altogether in the coupleness that my wife and I had built up over the years. Now I know there's three ways to do things: my way, her way, and His way - whereby we both "win" and grow together as He planned all along!

My prayer is that other men will be led to read this simple but powerful guide to married life, and that it will help them to grow with their wives in faith, hope and love. Whether it's given to a couple as a wedding present, or passed along by a friend who wants only the best for them in their golden years, its lessons are timeless and priceless.

Fred Holtslag
Retired Military Pilot
Vice-Chair of Living Water Arts Foundation
St. Albert, Alberta
Married 31 years

"Terry is an "Ordinary Guy" with a huge commitment to life, faith, and most of all to his wife Laura. Terry combines his artistic nature with his dogged determination to be practically engaged in the work/pleasure of marriage. As he puts it in his book; "I don't know how this is going to go, but I am in it to the end!" (p50)

Terry starts from the point of lifelong commitment and a determination to make both his life and marriage extraordinary! This straight shooting book combines motivation and practical tips for getting the most out of one's marriage."

Jack Mortensen
Director of Resource Development for Young Life of Canada
Calgary, Alberta
Married 38 years

Every now and then, someone comes along with a big "WAKE UP CALL". This someone is Terry Bachynski and he has succeeded in rousing husbands (and wives) out of the slumber of mediocracy and into the joy and delight of truly extraordinary marriages.

Bob and Beth Humphreys
Edmonton, Alberta
Married 33 years

It is impossible to read this book and not improve your marriage. The simple truths presented in this book have given me the opportunity to shine as a husband and enrich my own marriage. Quite honestly, this book should be mandatory reading for married men. It will improve your marriage and your life.

Dr. Stephen Goodwin
Edmonton, Alberta
Married 10 years

Terry and Laura are an extraordinary yet normal couple - they have four kids and complex lives. What's amazing to me is the clarity of their thought and practice that is well described in the book. As we understand how they think and act we can learn a great deal that will help us calm all the "crazymaking" issues that affect our marriages.

Terry's book is a great read, especially for men, who generally avoid reading books on marriage. He has fresh, foundational thinking that will have you saying – "that's a good idea – I should do that..." As I read of Terry's early learning I laughed out loud. Some things just cracked me up!

I think all men will relate and benefit.

John McNicoll, B.Ed., M.Th.
Western Divisional Director for Young Life of Canada
Edmonton, Alberta
Married 21 years

Love is patient, love is kind. It does not envy, it does not boast, it is not proud. It is not rude, it is not self-seeking, it is not easily angered, it keeps no record of wrongs. Love does not delight in evil but rejoices with the truth. It always protects, always trusts, always hopes, always perseveres. Love never fails.

1 Corinthians 13:4-8

ORDINARY GUY EXTRAORDINARY MARRIAGE

TERRY BACHYNSKI

Cover design and illustration by Lana Bachynski
Edited by family and friends
Cover photo by Fred Katz MPA - Fine Art Photography
            Edmonton, Alberta

ORDINARY GUY – EXTRAORDINARY MARRIAGE
© 2008 by Terry Bachynski

Distributed by
  JDEL Associates Ltd.
  #208, 4207 – 98th Street
  Edmonton, Alberta, Canada T6E 5R7
  Phone: 780.455.6710
  terry@ordinary-guy.com
  www.ordinary-guy.com

ISBN 978-1-897544-06-8

Fourth printing
Printed in Edmonton, Alberta, Canada

PUBLICATION ASSISTANCE AND DIGITAL PRINTING IN CANADA BY

For my bride, Laura

Preface – Why listen to me?

"The man who says his wife can't take a joke,
forgets that she took him."

-Oscar Wilde

I have a reason for writing this book. It is simple. Marriage has been the single most phenomenal, joyous, wonderful, impactful experience of my life. It continues to be so. Being married to Laura has given me every joy. I think it is great. I think marriage, as a relationship between two people, is the most profound way anyone can choose to spend their life. And, I think getting it right is very important. Not only that, by getting it right, there is no end to the pleasures that life can provide for the lucky couple who find each other and discover in their sharing what true marriage means. It is just the coolest thing ever.

That's why I am writing this book. I love my marriage. I love what is does for me. Quite frankly, I hear and see so much in other marriages where people are missing the boat. They are letting the greatest opportunity of their lives just disappear, dissolve, wash away, evaporate. They are strangling the joy out of the whole experience; sucking the fun right out of life by not taking time to figure it out. They are missing the opportunity to embrace a chance to elevate themselves to new levels of peace and happiness.

Does that sound sappy enough for you? Not exactly the stuff of Wednesday night late ice time locker room conversation – is it?

Here's the deal. I am an ordinary guy and I have an extraordinary marriage. Trust me. That's not my assessment. My marriage is fantastic. But, first I have to make a correction right now. It is not my marriage I am talking about. It's OUR marriage. Laura's and mine. From here on, out I will always talk about "our" and "we". I just don't think in the "me" and "my". And that's not some crap I am saying for the sake of this book. It's true. Our marriage is exceptional. That's what everyone tells us. For the longest time I never really thought about it in those terms. It was just how we lived, what we did, how we worked together and played together. It was just our life – together. Over the years Laura and I have been approached many times with questions. What is it with you two? What's different about you guys? How do you do it? I want what you've got. How do I do that?

For years, we just kind of laughed and said things like, "Thanks. Yeah we are really happy. We just have a lot of fun together." We tried to leave it at that; but, you know, some things just will not let go. For years and years people – individuals and couples – have come to one or both of us and asked us to just listen to them. We would go out for coffee or make a pot of tea and then begin to listen. Out would come long stories of pain and frustration and anger and fear and sadness and emptiness and desire and longing. It seemed many people, our friends and sometimes people we hardly knew, just wanted to share what they were experiencing in their marriage relationship and then, inevitably conclude with, "I want what you have. What do I do?" We even get calls from people we have never met. Someone else has seen their need and given them our name and number and invited them to just talk to us. So, we listen and we share.

On more than one occasion I have been sitting at my desk at work, just doing my thing and a colleague has come into my office, closed the door (always a sure fire sign this is not going to be a "Did you see the game last night?" conversation) and has said, "Do you have a few minutes to talk?" Inevitably that's the sign that it is not going to be a few minutes. It is going to be as long as it takes. What do you do in a situation like that? The answer is easy. You take as long as it takes. How can I do anything else? There is absolutely nothing in my work day that could possibly be more pressing or important than to respond positively to another person asking me for help. Now, if you are a cardiac surgeon and you are elbows deep in someone else's aorta, you probably have a justification for saying, "Can this wait until later?" But, my work generally is just not that urgent. When someone is in need, work can wait.

Many men have approached me over the years with this same plea for help. Constantly I have been encouraged to share my experiences and ideas about caring for your marriage with a broader audience. Every time I have just brushed the idea off. I have not been seeking a role as a marriage advisor or self-help guru. I shudder at the notion even now as I type these words on my laptop that I am even trying to record in these pages words of advice that men will read and take to heart and perhaps even try to implement. And it scares the crap out of me that I may be wrong. What I say or suggest may not work. Many people are walking through life in what anyone would say is a highly functioning relationship. They are not unhappy. Their marriage is not on the skids. Life is rolling along as expected. They have settled into a nice equilibrium of certainty, steadiness and hopefully, love. I believe there is opportunity for even these couples to expand their marriage into an exceptional relationship.

So, this book is for everyone – the happily married, the not-so-happily married and those who may be contemplating marriage. All I know is that the things I share with you in these pages are real. The stories are true. The ideas are honest and everything I tell you that works or does not work for me really does work or doesn't work, as the case may be.

One thing I have to be straight with you on. I am a Christian. You need to know that. My Catholic beliefs form the foundation of my life. It is through the lens of my faith that I view my world. My thoughts and opinions are fundamentally grounded in the truth that I believe and accept that Jesus Christ is my Lord and Savior. My wife, Laura, shares this faith with me. In fact, her faith is undoubtedly stronger and more reliable than mine. I count on her to keep me in line and strengthen me when my faith gets fragile. So, everything I have to say in this book comes from that foundation of Christian faith. However, I hope that what is shared here is relevant to everyone who desires to make their marriage the very best it can be.

Also, I am not a professional marriage counselor. I am not a psychologist, psychiatrist, M.D. or Ph.D. of the human relational dynamic. All the books I have seen about human relationships and the challenges and examination of the marriage relationship are written by professionally trained individuals with long resumes about studying human behavior and saving emotional lives. I have got none of that.

I have never read a marriage help book until this year. I just didn't care to do so. Never felt the need. I am reading them now though and I have to admit, it is interesting; but, I still don't believe I need these books. My marriage is great.

However, I am reading a lot now to educate myself on what is out there for guys who just might want some help with their marriage. Maybe I am wired wrong, but, if I was a guy who seriously wanted to get some help with my marriage, asking for help is the hardest thing to do. It is, however, step one and to get help, you have to ask for it. Guys don't even like asking for directions to a restaurant! How hard is it to finally admit we need help with something as personal as our marriage?

I am told that well over 80% of all marriage books are bought and read by women. I don't know who told me that, but it sounds like a good number and although I have not validated it, it seems right to me – at least within striking distance of right. Anyway, guys don't want to read this stuff (even though a lot of what I have been reading is pretty good. These Ph.D.'s and other experts do know their stuff.) Guys just want to cut to the chase. Give them some ideas about how they can address some of the stuff in their marriage that they would like to improve. They want help, not a third year psychology course on why the help will help.

I think if I can get you started with a couple of ideas about how you can immediately start impacting your marriage for the better, your pleasure in experiencing the improvement should motivate you to do more. Then, maybe you will read some of these other books... or better yet... just focus more energy on your marriage instead of waiting for someone else (aka: your wife) to do all the work.

I am just a guy – an ordinary guy. Because of that, I worry that putting myself out there as someone who should be listened to about this amazingly complicated thing called marriage is a bit on the risky side. To counter that concern I offer these as my credentials:

- I love my wife

- My wife loves me (that is not a guess – She told me so – today – in an e-mail – and I believe her)

- We have been married over twenty-five years and it is great

There's more to it than that. I'll get to it all eventually.

So, why should you listen to me? Well, because I think we all could use a little help and encouragement from time to time. Sometimes it is nice to know you are not alone, that what you have, are or will experience is not just your experience. Others, many others, have been through it before and I am offering one husband's view about what is important to us, Laura and me, in building and sustaining an extraordinary marriage.

I have a sincere desire to help other men enjoy the kind of remarkable relationship that is possible between you and your wife that I enjoy with mine. It is that simple and that honest. So, read on. Hopefully, you will find something in these pages that rings true for you. If you extract just one idea from this book that assists you in growing closer to your wife and nourishes your love for each other, then the whole effort is a success.

Terry Bachynski
May 2008

Acknowledgements

For years whenever I have been asked, "If you could do anything in the world and money was no object, what would you do?" my answer has been the same. I would write and speak about marriage. Finally, this year, after continuous encouragement from many people, I decided to try and do something about that. My 2008 New Year's resolution was to listen to God more and act on what He is telling me. And so, "Ordinary Guy – Extraordinary Marriage" began.

I began thinking about how I could advance this idea and soon friends and family were encouraging me to pursue speaking engagements and writing. This book represents the beginning of this effort to spend more of my time trying to help men and women experience what I have – an extraordinary marriage.

I have many people to thank for getting me this far. First, I have to thank my Mom and Dad, Joan and Ed Bachynski who really have been my model for a great marriage. I have learned so much from them. I also have to thank Mary Anne and Dennis Drew, my wife's parents who raised an absolutely spectacular daughter and allowed me to marry her. Their commitment to marriage has been a pleasure to observe these last thirty years as well.

Many, many friends have helped me write this book without ever knowing it because they have contributed to my experiences that have been used as raw material for the contents of this book. Some have been unwitting participants in my thought process as I have worked on this book because I would engage them in conversations about various aspects of the man/woman relationship and marriage and extract some really great thoughts and ideas that helped me advance my writing. So thank you Pam and Dave Pellizzari, Rose and Shaun MacNeil, Albert Felicitas, Debbie Parsons, Doug Johnson, Zane and Zoe Gulley, Kyle Scott, John Gulley, Cindy Gibson, Karim Zariffa, Jason Heisler, Khaled Saleh, Tara Hingley, Chris Fordham, Sue Lowell, Ellen Lauersen, Carolyn Terakita, Dave Spencer, Ross and Lynne Birtwistle, Adam Pekarsky, Richard and Brenda White, Tom Fenn and my dear departed friend, Catherine Anderson. Thanks to my Tuesday morning bible study buddies – Jack, David, Larry, Bruce, David, Ed, Peter, Doug, Don and others.

I especially have to thank the following people who, not only encouraged me, but also read drafts of the book and provided me with their wisdom and input into the final product. Special thanks to Marie Bridge and Richard Turner, Jackie and Rick Tiedemann, Tim Senger, Carolyn and Dave Ardell, Doug and Judy Kramer, John and Susan McNicoll, Betty Stevens-Guille, Maurice and Leanne Brunelle and Guy and Louise Croome. Your contributions and support in this project were wonderful. I always knew I could count on the generosity of our friends.

I want to thank my children, Jared, Darren, Lana and Emily for being my inspiration to pursue this project because they remind me everyday how important it is to stand as an example for the world that marriage is important. It is special and it must never be taken for granted. They make me want to be a better married person so that they can see that a married life is a wonderful way to spend your days on this earth.

A special thanks to Lana who has been a great help to me as we try to get this entire project off the ground. She designed the cover for this book, ran around and did a lot of research and leg work for me to get this project to print. She is also my photographer and graphic designer and she designed and built the www.ordinary-guy.com website. Thank you, Lana.

A special thanks to Tim Senger, too. He has been a terrific encouragement for me and has helped Lana on the website. Thanks so much, Tim.

And finally, and most significantly, I thank you, my beautiful bride, Laura, for all your support and love. It seems ridiculous that I am identified as the author of this book because, just like our extraordinary marriage, this book takes two – Laura and me. Nothing would be possible without you. You are the best part of me.

Contents

I am an Ordinary Guy – I can prove it!

"Marriage is like a phone call in the night:
first the ring, and then you wake up."

-Evelyn Hendrickson

I like sports. I like watching them. I like playing them. I like pretending I am better at them than I really am. I like to Monday morning quarterback the entire weekend of sports competitions with brilliant analysis of what I would have done on that play, who I would have put into the game at that critical moment, what play I would have run in the last minute of the game, or the right golf shot I would have played to win the championship. I hate asking for directions. I can putz around in the garage all day. I like to read the paper on Saturday morning, uninterrupted. I can feel real proud of how sharp I can get the lawn mower blade; but, I don't like cutting the lawn. I like action movies and I actually like a good romantic comedy, but I don't always like admitting that. I work hard at my business and try to provide a good life for my family. I've got a few hobbies that I enjoy when I have the time. I like nachos with all the trimmings and now, with the passage of time, I find I am telling more and more stories about victories of the past. When I try to pretend I am still young, I pull a lot more muscles. I can never find anything. I am just an ordinary guy.

The best part of me is this: I am married to Laura.

We have been married for over twenty-five years and we are still going strong. A lot has happened in the last quarter century that has challenged us. We have been poor. We have been "less poor". We have been healthy and we have struggled with illness and pain. We have had good times and bad. Almost sounds cliché, doesn't it? Well, it's marriage. It's life.

Let me tell you a little bit about all of this. First, the good stuff. We have four truly wonderful children. Jared is twenty-two. Darren is twenty-one. Our twins, Emily and Lana are nineteen. All are at various stages of the post-secondary education and they are a constant joy to us. I could talk about them for a long time, but I won't. You know why? Because this is a book about marriage, not parenting. I am sure the kids will come up from time to time, but for now, let's just say they are great.

The marriage is the thing for now. You'll get lots of stories about our experiences wrestling with this whole marriage thing throughout this book. I just want to lay down a brief foundation of experience for you now. Here are some of the highlights.

We know what it feels like to be:

- immeasurably happy and blessed with children, family and friends

- Completely broke with no food in the cupboard or rent money in the bank

- Unemployed for months at a time – more than once

- Struggling with severe and chronic illness and disability

- Saved by an angel when we are in distress

- Sick with worry and fear over a missing child

- Afraid and worried and stressed

- Reliant on the kindness of others just to get through another day

- Joyful

- Doubtful of our own abilities to go on

Sound familiar? In short, we are human and we have experienced a broad array of life's surprises. Oh, there is one more thing – Laura and I have an extraordinary marriage. It is wonderful, truly wonderful.

I believe everyone has the opportunity to enjoy an extraordinary marriage. I want you to have the chance to experience in your life the kind of joy and love we have in ours. You just have to want it and be prepared to work tirelessly everyday of your life for it.

Believe me, if you are sincerely committed to achieving it, you can have an extraordinary marriage. And, all the work you will have to do and choices you will have to make along the way will be well worth it. There is nothing on this earth that can compare to the joy of a wonderful marriage, my friend. I encourage you to put all else aside and focus on your marriage. Get it right, and everything else that truly matters will be possible.

Marriage – Why do it?

"Marriage has no guarantees. If that's what you're looking for, go live with a car battery."

-Erma Bombeck

Anything worth doing should scare the crap out of you.

A few weeks ago I was at a friend's home and we were sharing new music. Once a month my friend hosts a songwriter's circle in his home and generously invites a wide spectrum of songwriters – professionals, amateurs, established, aspiring, career focused and hobbyists – to come with a new piece of original music. You play your song for everyone and the group provides you with their feedback. The evening is very positive and constructive and, for many, intimidating because you are putting your creative efforts out there for others to critique.

I listened to my friend sing a new song that he had just written about the fear of performing in front of live audiences. The song, ultimately, spoke to much more than the fear of live performing. It was really about what matters. The lyric spoke about the feeling you get right down to your core when something is really important to you. It is so important that you have to get out there and pursue it. You have to chase that dream at all costs and to do so, you have to step outside your comfort zone.

Chasing your life's purpose can shake your confidence. In the broadest sense, committing your life to pursuing your core purpose – your soul's ambition – can be gut wrenching. It can cause you to re-think perhaps all of the choices you have made that have carried you to this point in your journey. It can force you to let go of some of your most prized emotional possessions – those walls of comfort, of self preservation, of safety that have perhaps helped define you. The decision that allows you to finally recognize, "This is it for me. This is what I am supposed to be doing with my life" eclipses all that other noise. None of that other stuff matters. Every other aspect of your life lines up behind this one thing because it is the most important and fulfilling thing you can do with this life of yours. Through it, everything else will find its place and each moment of your life will be enhanced. The pleasure of the sum total of your life will be magnified because it all fits within this one true thing. All of your decisions from this point forward will consider making this one thing better in your life because it is your priority.

This kind of commitment can rattle your emotions, cause you to lose sleep, infect you with self doubt. But, if it is what you are meant to do, you have to fight through all of that and go for it because, in the end, you have to. Does that sound like a vocation? Through all the self examination and excuses why you can't, your truth is that you have to.

Some of us struggle with discovering, recognizing, accepting and acting on what we truly are meant to be doing. I am not simply talking about what you do in your life. I am not talking about cash flow. I am not talking about satisfaction with the rhythm of your life, the creature comforts, the safety or, regretfully too often, the resignation that "this is as good as it gets". I am talking about fulfilling your life with what matters in a way that lifts you beyond the mundane consolation of compromise and regret. I am talking about the realization of joy in your life.

That's what my marriage is to me. That's what I want your marriage to be for you. Second only to my conscious decision to be a Christian, my decision to join Laura in marriage was the single most important decision I have and will ever make in my life. It is distressing beyond words to see how our society has minimized the magnitude of this decision. Popular social conscience encourages us to take the decision to marry lightly and casually. Marriage is viewed, remarkably, as disposable, replaceable, or even temporary as a matter of fiscal, domestic and sexual convenience.

Marriage is a vocation. In my religious tradition it is a sacrament. It is sacred. It is my covenant with God and this one woman. With naïve young minds and hearts, Laura and I accepted this burdened blessing to share one life with each other over twenty-five years ago. In that moment of promise, there was a love and commitment to each other that we would each take on our share of the burdens of this decision. In that moment, we embarked on a promise to build together something that we could not possibly achieve without each other, side by side, every day.

The experience has not been perfect. No, let me correct that. Our marriage has been perfect, but not in the sense of "without flaw". I have a different definition in this context. I am flawed. In more ways than I care to confess. We all have our warts. Even my wife, whom I adore, is not perfect. (Sorry, Sweetheart. It's true.) But, our marriage has been perfect *be-*

cause of all of its flaws. Not perfect in the sense of effortless, like some sort of divine paradise. It has been perfect because of the happiness and struggles, battles and wounds, healing and loving that it has provided for us. It has created for us the opportunity for joy and it has been up to us to work hard to capture that joy throughout this shared life.

Sometimes it scares me. It shakes my self confidence. I lose sleep. I worry. I get angry, anxious and ambivalent. I get tired, bored and lonely. I have felt cramped, suffocated, starved for self indulgence. I have fought the urge to take care of me first countless times over the years. Sometimes I have lost that battle. On balance, I think I can say we are winning the war. The evidence is in the extraordinary relationship Laura and I have and our unshaken confidence that we are one.

Everything in our life springs from this core truth in us – we are one. We actively love each other and we are dedicated to each other completely.

Let me back up and set this up for you a little. I am a farm boy, raised in southwestern Ontario. We lived on a farm a couple of miles from town. That's what we called them then – miles. I guess now it would be more Canadian to say "a few kilometers", but, I still like using miles. Pretty typical child-hood. Worked hard. Played hard. There was always work to do at our house. That was our fun. My mom and dad were like a well oiled marital machine. They worked side by side their whole lives, providing their five children with daily, real time examples of how a husband and wife can build a life together raising a small herd of children within a framework of unambiguous rules and priorities and they never lost the fun in their life. My memories of my parents together are two people who worked hard, showed each other affection, teased and tickled, laughed and cried, argued and made up, all in the wide open for their children to see.

It was wonderful. No matter what was going on in our family's life, success or struggle, sorrow or laughter, there was never any doubt in my mind that my mom and dad loved each other and would do anything for each other. What a great example to witness every day. I know things were not perfect. They had their struggles as all couples do; but, the struggles do not fill my memories. My memory is of a father and mother who always loved each other.

I was lucky. I know. I am not blind to the realities that far too many people do not grow up in what I consider to be a "blessed" family life. We were fortunate beyond measure because we had great parents. And, in no small measure, as I look back with the analytical eye of adulthood, our parents were great parents because they were first, a great couple. They still are.

Thankfully they are still kicking, healthy and happy. My dad likes to pretend that he has become this crazy curmudgeon and my mom puts up with it, occasionally admonishing him with a little "love slap". A good example of a love slap is when Dad says something particularly ridiculous about just about anything (and that is exactly what he does just to get a reaction from anyone who's listening), Mom will come back with, "What the heck are you talking about?" or "You're being ridiculous." And then she'll give a little chuckle and he'll sit there with a little look of satisfaction – a half smirk on his face – because he got a little rise out of her. It's a mini-scene that has been played out thousands of times over the fifty-three years of their marriage. And there is no sign of it stopping now.

So, I was lucky. But, I do not hold that up as an excuse or an explanation of why I continue to be very lucky because I have a great marriage. Many people have risen above their less fortunate childhood to become wonderful husbands and wives. Certainly having a great role model is a help. But it's not required.

For proof, I do not have to look any further than my own father again. He was not so lucky as a child. Orphaned at an early age, he spent his youth in and out of "The Manor" (also known as the orphanage), shipped from foster home to foster home. He would run away a lot, get caught and the cycle of Manor, foster home, run away would continue well into his mid teens. He just never had a family. Then, in his mid teens, he was shipped to another foster home. In that community he met my mom.

They dated and much to the chagrin of my mom's parents, eight years later, they married. Seven years later they had five children. I was number three. Somehow, notwithstanding a complete lack of positive parental influence in his life, my father became a loving and devoted husband, completely dedicated to his wife and children. Kind, stern, wise, compassionate, committed. He was (and is) all of these and more. I could equally say all the same things about my mom. They are such an integrated team. No, "team" is not the right word. Their two lives really did become one, just as the wedding vows promise. To call them an "integrated team" is to somehow diminish the truth. They are one. They are married. Truly married. And to understand that, and better yet, to witness that, is, without a doubt, a most spectacular life experience.

As for myself, well, I met Laura in November 1977. We were both auditioning for a local theatre company and ended up being cast in the show. We had small roles in the play, a musical called *Finian's Rainbow*, and we were understudies for the leads. I was hooked on her the minute I laid my eyes on her when she stood up to audition. By the end of the show, we were dating.

Our courtship was, to say the least, unusual. We never lived in the same community until we were married. Laura lived in a town about twenty miles from our farm. We dated for a few months and then Laura took off across the country with three girlfriends for their great adventure. They went to Calgary for the summer of 1978. Toward the end of the summer, Laura came home, but two weeks after her return, I went away to university. For the next three years we saw each other at Thanksgiving, Christmas, spring break, Easter and during summer holidays. When I graduated from university, I asked Laura to marry me. She said "yes". Two weeks later it was my turn to move to Calgary to begin my career. Laura stayed back to finish her last year of university. Fourteen and a half months later, I returned to Ontario and five days later we were married. That was almost twenty-six years ago.

A few weeks after our wedding I was standing before a judge in court. Now don't get the wrong idea. I was there in a professional capacity. The last step for a law student in becoming a lawyer is to be sworn in as a member of the legal profession before a judge once you have completed all of the requirements. That's where I was in my career. On that day I stood before the judge, having been sponsored by a senior member of the law firm where I was employed who recommended my acceptance into the profession to the judge. The judge's final requirement was to issue the oath of membership to me and I was in. But, before the judge did this, he asked me one question. "Mr. Bachynski," he said. "What do you want to accomplish in your life?" My mind raced for something to say about the professional responsibilities and the oath of membership I was about to take. After a moment, I took a breath and answered, "I want to make my wife happy."

That really was the promise I made only three weeks earlier at our wedding. Laura often describes her promise to me as this. It is her job to get me to heaven. I like that, because certainly I need all the help I can get and I am pretty sure I could not get there on my own.

So, what do those promises mean really? Make her happy. Help him get to heaven. So easy to say. Kind of sweet and sickening isn't it? You could just hear the day time talk show audience all saying "Aaaah" all together as they cut to commercial. Well, fundamentally, it's a frame of mind. Promises like these greatly define your behavior. They do not stop you from making mistakes. However, if it is true that I am really committed to the goal of making my wife happy, I will most certainly make different decisions than if I was of the view that I will keep her clothed and fed and housed and free of abuse and expect her to figure out her own happiness. My goal should define how I will live this married life.

I am really talking about here are the marriage vows, translated into the phrase "keeping her happy". It is a kind of short hand way to talk about how this lifelong commitment should impact a person's attitude, priorities, choices and behaviors. "Keeping her happy" means all of that.

So, let's talk about all of that. They all are really important and how you view them and how they translate to action and attitude in your life will certainly impact the quality of your marriage.

Priority is a big subject. I am going to spend some more time on this later. However, get your priorities right and a lot of other stuff falls into place. Commit to those priorities and you will constantly self-correct when you wander away from them. The more committed you are to your priorities, the more you can build a track record of behavior around these priorities, the quicker that self-correction will come with the regular flow of your life's experiences. That's not to say new experiences, new temptations, new challenges throughout your life will not be hard. Sometimes they can be crippling. And the old temptations of your single life and challenges that test your personal weaknesses never just die and go away. They have a way of repeatedly showing up over and over again. However, with our priorities straight, we find strength in dealing with whatever life throws at us.

Life's biggest questions all come with easy answers. Our priorities help us to know when we have to dig in and choose the tough answers because they are the right ones in the greater scope of things, even though at the time of making those choices, we would really like to be doing something else – the easy answer – the "burger and fries for the soul" answer that tastes great right now, but will not really sustain or nourish us in the long haul, and, in fact, (to strain the food consumption analogy a bit) may kind of upset our systems as it works its way through. At some point we regret the greasy burger and fries and wish we would have opted for a healthier choice.

In short, being selfish just doesn't build a very fulfilling life. And everything is incremental. Little decisions that start down a path of behavior have a way of multiplying, accumulating and defining us. So, we have to be diligent all the time to make sure we are moving in the right direction. It's the little daily decisions of our lives that really get us to the finish line. The big decisions are relatively rare and infrequent. If we have not established a pattern of how we make our little decisions, when the big ones come along, they can throw us for a loop. Making good decisions – note I did not say perfect decisions – on the little things, helps build behavior that will serve us well when dealing with the big ones.

There are literally thousands of examples of small decisions that we make in our daily lives that helps us on our way. Specifically, with our marriages, we make them all the time. Often, probably most often, we make these decisions without even thinking about them. That can be a problem. We have to think about them to make sure our marriage is always in front of us. To increase the likelihood that we will make good decisions, we need to learn as much as we can and understand as much as we can about that person with whom we share our life.

Sometimes trying to understand your wife is like trying to learn a new language. There is no short cut to that. You have to invest the time to learn the language. You don't have to necessarily be fully fluent in German to find your way around Germany, but having a functional understanding of the language sure makes it a lot easier. So it is with your relationship with your wife. The more you understand her, the easier it is going to be to build a life with her. Sometimes you may even have to ask for instructions. Lots of times you are being offered instructions and you don't even know it. My advice is "Clue in!"

Human relationship is complicated. Marriage is one of the toughest thing we undertake in this life – to hang on to one relationship and make it a focus of our entire life. It is a big challenge. A marriage is profoundly complicated. Every nuance of two individuals, every quirk and talent, prejudice and point of view has to be accommodated and respected. Individual strengths must be nurtured and their weaknesses protected in a daily ebb and flow of human emotion and experience. Ideally, it is happy and fulfilling. Without care and attention, this relationship can become bogged down in frustration and disappointment. In the worse case it results in two lives lost and isolated.

Well, that's no good. Let's focus on the positive. Let's find some ways to maximize the opportunity for success. That's what I think picking the right priorities and sticking with them does for marriage. Without agreed priorities, how do you deal with the challenges of the marriage? How do you make decisions?

Priority #1 – the marriage is number one. How's that for simple. There is no alternative really. Is there? If you expect your marriage to survive all manner of challenges and threats, without making it the number one priority in your life, that expectation is pretty much a foolhardy hope. It is like relying on winning the lottery for your retirement plan. It is possible, but a bit of a long shot. The marriage priority creates the foundation for so many of your choices. It comes into play with everything. Are you going to take that promotion in another city? First question – Is it good for the marriage? Then consider the ramifications of the move for other things like impacts to children, their school situation, your spouse's career and relationships with friends and extended family.

Are you going to sign the kids up for every extracurricular activity you can find and run yourself ragged running your parent taxi service? First question – Is it good for the marriage? Then consider if it is good for the kids.

Are you going to buy that wide screen TV so that you can watch a lot more sports in HD? First question – Is it good for the marriage? Then consider if you can afford it.

Does your wife go away for the weekend with the girls? First question – is it good for the marriage? Then consider if it is good timing, if it's good for her relationships with her friends?

Want to go to that neighborhood barbeque on Friday night? First question – (I think you know it by now). Then consider the options of just spending time together with each other to catch up on your busy week and re-connecting as a husband and wife.

Are you going to put a TV in the bedroom? First question – ...You get the point.

There are a lot of other priorities in our lives. I know that. Having a family and providing for the family. Raising great children and giving them every opportunity to realize their full potential. Regular, reliable cash flow for the family. Buying and paying for a home. Charitable giving. Volunteerism. Caring for aging parents. The list goes on and on.

I think we get confused with what are true priorities and what are goals or objectives or just things to do. Without really focusing on a few – and I do mean very few – priorities that help direct our lives, then I think we can get eaten up with the busy-ness that life throws at us every day.

Our marriage has always been a priority for us. Our relationship as a man and woman, husband and wife is something Laura and I have always focused on. We have always carved out a part of our life together where no one else is invited. All through this book you will read examples of that. For one example, we protect Friday nights just for us. It is our date night. No one else is invited. You'll read more about that later.

Another example – our bedroom is OUR room. No kids invited. Even with new born babies in our family and my wife nursing them, the baby was in his or her own room as soon as possible. For middle of the night feedings, we shared the task of getting the baby for his or her or their (twins) feeding. However, our bedroom has always been our room.

In our life, we had a major event that helped define this as our priority and forced us to really make it a central tenement in our relationship that has stood up for all of our marriage. Early in our marriage our wedding vows got exercised in a significant way. We have been tested on the "for richer or poorer" part and the "good times and bad" part. But, a significant chapter in our marriage was the "in sickness and in health" part of the marriage vows.

When we were first married, Laura was building a career as a stage actress. She was exceptionally talented. She still is. (I am not just saying that because she is my wife and I know she will read this. It is true.) Right after our honeymoon, my new wife joined me in Calgary where I had been working as a newly minted law school graduate for the past year. Soon Laura was landing acting jobs in many of the theatre companies and stage productions around town. A real triple threat, Laura could sing and dance and act and it was great to see her enjoy herself and pursue her dream of being a professional actress.

Laura's acting endeavors continued through the child bearing years. We had four children in three years. The first two were boys and the second two were identical twin girls. During this time, Laura's acting career did not go on hold, but, for obvious reasons, there were breaks. Once the girls were born and we survived those early months of no sleep and adjusting to the new routine of a house with four children, Laura began working on getting back into shape and returning to her professional pursuits in the theatre.

We had an understanding that my career was the main stay as far as financial security for the family. But even that got tested early in our marriage when, quite unexpectedly and on Laura's birthday, nine months after our wedding, I was down sized out of my law firm. With the economy in the tank and no one hiring, I opened my own law office after months of looking for work. I made no money the first year. Well, actually, my accountant at the time told me I made $3,000 that first year. I remember asking her, "If I made $3,000, where is it cuz I don't have it." We survived mostly on what Laura made as a part time day care worker. Talk about money being tight! But, that's another story – just one of the "for richer or poorer" stories of our life together. This story is about what happened after our daughters were born.

Once we settled into the "sanity" of a home with four young children, my legal practice on a little more solid foundation than when it started, Laura began to exercise. She wanted to get back into good shape and return to the theatre. Almost immediately upon launching into her exercise regime, Laura hurt herself. She pulled a groin muscle and it seemed that it would never heal. For nine months she experienced this nagging pain in her groin that prevented her from getting back into dancing shape. It was really frustrating for her.

Then, one day, Laura was reading the Saturday morning newspaper and pointed out an article of interest and asked me to read it. The article was all about arthritis and it talked about how it is not just a disease of the aged. Anyone can get arthritis and it can be very crippling. The article described how osteoarthritis can attack specific joints, like the hips and can cause chronic pain. People with this disease may even mistake the pain in the joint as a pulled groin muscle because in the early stages, that is what it can feel like.

When I finished the article I looked up and said to Laura, "This is you." It was like the author of the article had been following Laura around for the last nine months, recording her pain and discomfort. "This is exactly you." A doctor's appointment was made. Our family doctor sent us to see an arthritis specialist. The specialist had X-rays of Laura's hips done. All of this took a few more months and the whole time, Laura's "groin injury" persisted. Finally, the specialist confirmed that Laura had advanced osteoarthritis in both hips. It was just a matter of time before both hips would eventually wear out and she would need hip replacement surgery.

What? That seemed ridiculous. Laura was thirty years old at the time – hardly your poster child for advanced osteoarthritis and hip replacements. True, our doctor told us, it is uncommon for someone so young to have this type of arthritis, but not unheard of. We were referred to an orthopedic surgeon who would take care of us from that point forward. We went back home with a prescription for pain management and were told to manage it as best we could. Time would tell what would be the next steps.

Well, time did tell and all too fast. Laura's pain escalated. Numerous pain relief medications and combinations of pills were tried to find something that would take the edge off the pain. Laura suffered with side effects from these medications – not only physical side effects, but emotional side effects. After our meeting with the specialist, Laura's mobility degraded in what can only be described as a remarkable way. This young, active, physically fit, professional dancer and actress soon needed a cane to walk around – then two canes – then crutches. Within nine months of being diagnosed with her arthritis, we went shopping for a wheelchair. For the next five years Laura's arthritis was so severe that she could not stand or walk even ten feet unaided. The drugs she needed to manage her pain became stronger and stronger and the ripple effect of that required more medications to deal with protecting her stomach and intestine linings from being eaten away by the other drugs. She could not dress herself completely. She could not run to pick up the kids, cook or care for her family the way she wanted to. She could not get up and down stairs or get in and out of the family van unaided. She could not wash her feet, clip her toe nails or drive a car.

We had to make all kinds of accommodations and changes to facilitate Laura's condition. We moved houses. We left our two-story, heritage home in an old inner city neighborhood for a bungalow in suburbia. Wheel chair ramps, handicap accessible fixtures in the bathroom, special furniture for Laura all came into our life. I changed careers. Rather than running my own, now thriving law practice (a time consuming enterprise) I took a job as a staff lawyer with a company, making less money than I was in my private practice. This gave me more routine hours that allowed for more predictability in our home. Also, the corporate job came with medical and dental benefits. Something we just did not have when I was self employed.

Everything in our life had to get done differently. So, things that may have been on a higher priority BA (before arthritis) were less important AA (after arthritis). Dust didn't get dusted quite so often. Rugs didn't get vacuumed all the time. Laundry piled up and I got to it sometimes in the middle of the night or on the weekend. We arranged for our groceries to be delivered.

Going to the mall, or anywhere in public, as a family was a major undertaking. I would push Laura. Jared, our oldest, was three or four years old. He would push his baby sisters in their stroller while Darren, our two year old, would sit on

Laura's lap or just walk along side hanging on. I am sure we made quite the family picture.

Through all of this I think I was basically shell shocked. I just kept on going, doing what had to be done to keep things going. We had a lot of help. We had support from friends and our faith community and the appreciation for the words "in sickness" as a part of the marriage vows was truly brought home. I have to admit that when I thought about the concept of "in sickness and in health" prior to this experience, I mostly considered taking care of Laura when she got knocked down with the flu for a couple days or the inevitable decline of our physical health that comes with living a long, long life. I never really thought about having a young bride disabled with arthritis and restricted to a wheel chair as a part of a young family with four children under the age of four. That just did not occur to me until the moment I found myself in that situation.

The whole situation struck home for me like a punch in the gut the day I went to the motor vehicle registry office with a doctor's certificate to pick up a handicapped parking sticker for our family van. I remember standing at the counter of the registry office. A young registry office employee with bleached blonde hair with black roots, wearing skin tight white jeans and pink lipstick, making a cracking sound with her bubble gum on every other chew and looking completely bored, finished with a customer and without even looking up said, "Next." I walked up to the counter. She looked up at me, but didn't say anything. Just waited for me to tell her what I wanted.

I began to tremble, handed her the doctor's note and said, "a handicapped parking sticker please." But the "please" was silent. My mouth moved, but nothing came out. I was shaking, unable to talk and I began to weep.

She immediately went into a slow motion, bored bureaucrat routine of retrieving the appropriate forms and asking for my identification and car registration documentation. She completed the forms, passed them to me for my signature, took my money and handed me the plastic rear view mirror symbol placard, my copy of the registration forms and my receipt and then said, "Next." She never looked at me, perhaps avoiding my obvious emotional distress. I never got the sense she was being sensitive to my condition. She just looked bored.

I left the registry office, got back in the van and sat there in the parking lot, crying. For about thirty minutes I just sat there, unable to comprehend what had happened to us. Why did my wife get hit with this disabling condition? How was I supposed to handle these four little children and care for a bride who could not even trim her own toe nails? This was not what I signed up for.

Then, suddenly, the tears stopped. An overwhelming realization came over me. This was exactly what I had signed up for. This was everything I signed up for. In sickness and in health. Everything I asked for from Laura and everything I promised her on our wedding day was right there in front of me. I promised to love her no matter what. She promised me the same. Nothing had changed. The choice right in that moment for me was to put up and shut up. Did I mean it when I declared my promise to her? Or was I only in it for the good days? In a millisecond, I woke up. I had pushed myself for months worrying about what all of this change in my wife's physical abilities would mean to our family, to our marriage. In many ways I think I was just denying it all, pushing the reality of the situation in the background while I simply pushed on with the reality of getting through the day. I never let the emotions of frustration, disappointment, anger, resentment or feelings of being overwhelmed and ripped off come forward. Selfishness and self pity and all other manner of natural human responses to a situation unplanned and unwanted overtook me and for thirty minutes in my car in the parking lot of the motor vehicle registry office I cried and screamed and cursed and wallowed in "why me?"

And in an instant it was over. This was my marriage. This circumstance was our life – the life intended for us – and my promise to spend the rest of my life making my wife happy came back to me. I drove away talking to myself and saying, "Never again. Never again will I doubt my promise to love this woman all the days of my life. To love her, to actively love her in that moment meant to never regret my situation, but to embrace the gift of this woman in my life and all that she brings to my life. To love her in the face of this challenge is to ensure that I never let her feel that her physical limita-tions in any way negatively impact the quality of our life or the depth of my commitment to our happiness together. My job is to ensure that when she does feel that way, depressed, sad and disappointed with herself and the circumstance that she didn't ask for, that I work to lift her up and make sure she knows that she is loved, that we are happy, that our children have a wonderful mother and that I have the best wife any man could ever ask for.

It is easy to actively love when you are riding the road of life's success. To love when life is letting you down is the test of every marriage.

I drove away from the registry office with clarity of purpose. I had doubted. I had forgotten. I had questioned. I was worn down and sick of the grind. I had lost the truth of my marriage vows. Finally, all of that natural human emotion just exploded out of me. In thirty minutes it was spent. It was gone. Clarity and commitment had re-established itself in me and I never doubted again. Whatever the road ahead would bring, Laura and I were going to face it together and through it all, we would love each other.

We were in our early thirty's with four very young children. For the next several years Laura would face all of the physical and emotional challenges of her limitations. Five years after buying that wheelchair, Laura had one of her hips replaced. Eighteen months later, the second hip was also replaced. She learned to walk again. Slowly she regained her strength. That was twelve years ago. She still needs medications to manage her pain and deals with physical limitations every day, but she is mobile. She is walking and a few years ago I surprised her with a gift of ballroom dancing lessons. And we danced.

Talk about a wake-up call to getting your life's priorities straight. It can be hard to keep clear on what is really important when everything is going so well. Careers are on cruise. Everyone is healthy. Success and fortune await us with every new day. In times like this, everything seems possible and over time it can become not only expected, but an entitlement.

Success is a seductive thing. It is hard to say "no" when everything is possible and available. Life's wake up calls are wonderful opportunities. They force us to take account and choose. What matters? What are our priorities? What can we discard because it is not important? How do we choose? Priorities. Knowing what they are and knowing that they hold true in all circumstances can help us focus on the things that matter. When we do that, I have found, the spectrum of available options, although always there, holds less temptation and the right choice quickly comes to the front of the line.

So, what are the "right" magical priorities? I have already told you my answer to that one. For you, they may be different. They can be different for everyone. They should be. There are many recipes for successful marriages. I do not want to tell you what should be important to you.

For me, the priorities list is very short. My God. My wife. My family. Everything else lines up behind those three priorities. It works for me. What really works is that Laura shares these priorities in the same order. Our decisions are all considered within this framework. I like the fact that the priority list is short. Too many and the decision process can get more complicated. I find that every other consideration really is of little importance. When we are focused on our priorities, our choices become fewer and the decision often becomes clearer. It is also a lot easier to live with a decision that may not necessarily be the thing that I want right now, but I know the decision is the right one. As a result, the "I want" option is easier to let go of without regret.

Sure, we get it wrong from time to time. Last I checked I was as flawed as the next guy. Fortunately, together Laura and I always help each other along the way. We encourage, correct, gently steer and guide each other. We help each other. We work together. We can lift each other up and, unified, we can build a marriage and a life that is worth living.

Because of this I can say that I do not sacrifice in my marriage. I choose. Sacrifice implies regret. I do not regret or look for that greener patch of grass on the other side of the fence. I am happy with the patch of grass I have on my side of the fence including all of its dandelions and clover and weeds. I don't need an Augusta National fairway to be happy. What's the fun in that kind of unnatural perfection?

We all know that no matter where we are there are green and brown patches everywhere. With our priorities clear, I can say that our decisions reflect my preferences because my preference always is the option that best fits with our shared priorities. In that way, I am always getting what I really want. I am not walking away from something that I really want. I am walking toward my choice. It is not sacrifice to say "no" to the other options. They are less favorable to me. With our shared priorities of God, marriage and family, Laura and I build a life focused on those things most important to us.

These priorities guide us and define our behaviors and our choices. They can also highlight our shortcomings.

Here is how these priorities factor into a real life decision that I have faced many times. Every spring when the snow is melting and the golf courses are opening, I think about getting a membership at a golf course. I love golf. I do not golf very much. I used to when I was a teenager and an annual membership cost fifty dollars at the local golf course. For that, I could knock the ball around as much as I wanted. But, marriage, career, mortgage, retirement plans, savings, university costs all seem to take priority over the golf membership. But, every spring, I think about it again. Is this the year that I finally dish out the cash to join a golf club?

Well, for years, the choice was easy. I could fantasize about it all that I wanted, but the reality was we just could not afford it. So, although I dreamt about it, joining a golf club was never a realistic possibility. During those years, groceries and mortgage payments were the priorities. I guess choosing food and a home for my family over a golf membership for me would in the framework of my "God-Marriage-Family" priority list be an obvious choice. But today, that choice is not as obvious.

We have been blessed with a good life. Enough money for groceries is not an issue. We own our home. We have been responsible in the planning for our children's education and our retirement. We can afford a golf membership. It is now a decision that is considered in a completely different reality. Now we can do this. The question now is – should we? So many times I have found that the decisions we make today are not a question of "Can we do this?" but "Should we do this?" Just because you *can* does not mean you *should.*

A golf membership, although it would satisfy a long standing desire on my part, in reality, still doesn't make sense for us. The truth is I would want to use the membership and spend much more time at the golf course than I should at this time in my life. Now that I've got it, I have to use it. Right? Feelings of entitlement and "my turn" could creep into my behavior. Laura would join me, of course, occasionally, but she does not have the same love of the game as I do and her physical limitations just would not let her golf as much as I could. It also takes a lot of time to play a round of golf. With travel to and from the course and the round itself, even without any post round socialization, a round of golf eats up the better part of a whole day.

With my work, I travel a lot. I am away from my family a lot. A golf membership would, quite frankly, take me away from them even more. Two of our children, although young adults, still live with us. We are still their parents and there is work yet to be done there. They need our attention as much now as ever. How can I do that if I am on the golf course?

In the final analysis, measuring the golf membership today against our priorities, it is still not something we would choose at this time. It will come, someday, I know. But not yet. So, I am happy getting out to the public golf courses in our community and enjoying the occasional round of golf through the summer months. Someday the time may be right for the golf membership. Someday that decision may fit with our priorities. I am happy to wait to see if it ever comes around.

Today, I am happy to say "no" to something that is clearly within our scope of possibility because even though we can do this, we choose not to. Within the framework of our decision-making and our clearly understood and agreed priorities, there is no regret. How can I regret the decision when I am doing what I choose to do because the choice supports what is most important to us? In this way I am doing exactly what I want to do. I am – correction – *we are* making choices that we believe will enrich and support our marriage. Those are the best decisions we can make and we know from experience that they will pay us back with more happiness in this shared life.

Love, Honor and Obey! YIKES!

"Marriage: A legal or religious ceremony by which two persons of the opposite sex solemnly agree to harass and spy on each other for ninety-nine years, or until death do them join."

-Elbert Hubbard

I'm not a big fan of homemade wedding vows. I have been to a lot of weddings when, after the vows have been exchanged, you kind of look at each other and say, "Huh? Are they married?" How can you tell sometimes? I know he is her sunshine on a rainy day and she is his spring blossom blooming in the fresh forest glade in the early morning dew, but I can't tell for sure from that if they are married. I guess they got married during the part where they promised to be each other's best friend and walk barefoot through the white sandy beach of life through low tide, through high tide, in the crashing waves and wind and through the calm stillness of life's sunsets.

Our wedding vows were pretty traditional.

"I, Terry, take you, Laura, to be my lawfully wedded wife. I promise to be true to you in good times and in bad, for

r, for poorer, in sickness and health, to have and to
hold from this day forward 'til death we do part. I promise to love you and honor you all the days of my life."

That's it. That is my promise. It is clear. It is concise. It is all
encompassing and, if understood and taken to heart, it has,
does and will define my priorities, my choices, my behaviors,
my mistakes, my apologies, my triumphs and my celebrations every moment of my life. With all of that relying on the
clarity of my promise at the beginning of this journey with
my new wife, I am happy that the vow is this brief and this
clear and this absolute.

Over the course of time my understanding of these words
has enhanced and improved. And, there are many things yet
to learn. Every one of the promises contained in this brief
statement of vows is powerful. They have literally saved me
from making some really poor decisions. Decisions that I
would not only regret immediately upon making them, but
also decisions that could burden me for a long, long time.
And, they continue to direct me every day. Although these
words do not roll through my head every day, they are there,
always influencing, always encouraging, and always nudg-
ing me. Like my wife, these promises give me the opportunity to be a better person every day. They encourage me to
work to become the kind of person I would have no hope of
being if I had never taken these vows. I cherish them and rely
upon them, like a touchstone, throughout my life.

This is a little bit about what I understand and believe at this
stage of my life, having walked the last twenty-five years en-
deavoring to fulfill the promises I made before my God, my
bride, my priest, my family and my friends.

Our marriage is my vocation. It is more than a legal obligation. It is a blessing, a gift from my God. It is not a domes-

tic arrangement or financial bargain. It is a sacred trust. It is not a one-time thing, generated to kick off a great party with food, wine, dancing, tossed bouquets and garters. It is a promise to dig in and work at this one thing for the rest of my life. It is surrendering my singleness, cashing it in for something greater. It is not giving up on my individuality or independence. It is a promise to identify my individuality and independence within the framework of a shared life.

I am always stunned when I hear things like, "I didn't sign up for this" when things aren't going the way you think they should. Well, here's the wake up call, my friend. Yes, you did. That's exactly what you signed up for. That's why we say "'til death we do part". Tough times are when the marriage vows are most demanding. Knowing and accepting what you signed up for in these times is critical. It is then that we can perhaps most clearly show that we actively love our wives. It is no time to cut and run and look for an easier way. Too many marriages seem to falter and fail because there is no staying power when it gets tough.

Marriage is a contact sport, my friend – so , wear your pads. It is not for the faint of heart. It is not for the meek or the unsure. Think about what we promise when we make those vows. These promises require us to keep working relentlessly at this single relationship above all others. When we make these vows, we are committing our life to a single purpose, a single priority – our marriage. Nothing comes before it except our relationship with our God. Not our children, our careers, our friends or extended family. This one relationship with this one woman is *the priority* against which all other decisions and relationships are measured.

The truth is, if we get this one right (and note I did not say "perfect"), then the whole world of possibilities in every other aspect of our life opens up for us with endless depth and color and dimension. I guarantee you, get the marriage piece of your life firing on all cylinders and the rest of your life will explode with richness.

Think about it. This is just practical and true. How can you excel in your career if your marriage is in turmoil? How can you love your children and enjoy your relationship with them to the fullest if you are distracted by the disintegration of your relationship with your wife? How can you enjoy your friendships, laugh and joke and play, when your mind is weary with the turmoil hidden behind the façade of a happy home?

You can't. That's the reality. Those of us who have been there know this. Those of us who have survived this experience also know it is worth it. The reality is that this is a promise of a lifetime commitment to stand firm together and build a single life together. We all falter. We all fall short. We all screw up. We are human after all. So, what do we do about it? We have choices. We can use our imperfection as an excuse or rationalization for failure. We can wallow in our mistakes. We can lean on the reality of our imperfect humanity, that flawed beauty of our human nature. We can let it fester, let it dominate our thinking and feeling, let it erode our commitment and confidence in our decisions. If it goes on long enough and is allowed to feed the seeds of doubt that are planted and sprout in our hearts and minds all the time, then these elements of our human nature can spark the flash fire of destruction that can scorch the relationship bare, perhaps never to recover.

OR...

We can forgive. We can dig in. We can accept all of our personal flaws and those of our spouse and say, "I stand by my vows. I stand by my promise." We can rely on our faith and believe that the greater prize of a single married life together is a greater goal than succumbing to the interruptions of harmony that are inevitable to arise numerous times over the course of decades that add up to a life together.

Think about the vows carefully. They are actions, not feelings. The vows require us to act in certain ways. We promise to love, not to "be in love" for the rest of our lives. It is a verb, not a noun. My vows require me to step up to the plate when in a precise circumstance I may not like my wife very much. I have to remind myself to love her and act accordingly.

I am constantly reminded of St. Augustine's instructions to me. "Love God and do as you please." (I am paraphrasing.) What is clear to me from this is that St. Augustine is revealing to us that if we choose to love (an action) God first, then the choices available to "do as we please" quickly define the appropriate options. If we love God first, and then consider all of our options, many of those options would quickly fall away because they would not be consistent with loving God. Only those choices that honor the intent or support the action of loving God could possibly be considered.

And so it is with the marriage vows. I promised to love Laura always. I promised to honor (again, a verb) her all the days of my life. If this stands as my priority in my life here on earth, then the choices available to fill the moments of my life with other actions, commitments, promises all must fall within the framework of my primary promise to first love her. I love Laura and then I do as I please – always in that order.

One of the toughest times to really keep the wedding vows squarely in front of you to guide you is when you don't really like your wife very much. This happens. It is, hopefully, short lived. But it happens. During times of conflict and disagreement, honoring the vows can be a real challenge. Times of "poorer" and "sickness" and "bad times" are the real test periods. And they all happen in the life of a marriage. They certainly have in our marriage as you will discover throughout the pages of this book. It is in these moments that we have to be most diligent. Our family has survived extended periods of sickness that have greatly influenced the entire rhythm of our family life. It has impacted where and how we live out of pure necessity. It has impacted career and lifestyle decisions.

We have been broke – very broke – more than once. That is not pleasant. My heart goes out to others who face these challenges. It is so easy to lose your focus on what matters when you are worried about next month's rent or this week's groceries. My heart also rejoices for those I have seen bravely stand firm together and survive these challenges.

Keeping the marriage vows is hard. Quite frankly, they get in the way quite a bit when I want to do something just for myself. Whenever I feel like just indulging me, my vows challenge me. Whenever I feel like "it's my turn" for once, my vows hit me over the head and force me to take a second look at my choices. Sometimes, I just want to do something for me. I don't want the responsibility. I don't want to have to worry about "the plan" for our future. I want to go out and spend some money on something that is a complete and utter waste of time and I want to enjoy it without regret, without guilt, without excuse or explanation or qualification. I just want it. I want it. I want it.

Then the light bulb comes back on. You know that expression about the great big elephant in the living room? It is so big and so obvious that you just cannot ignore it. You cannot get around it. You have to deal with it. In times like these, the great big elephant is my promise. I made a promise to love Laura first. I made a promise to honor her all the days of my life. How is indulging me an act of first loving her? How is feeding my selfish ego or desires an act of first honoring her?

The toughest times are the times when no one is watching. We have all been there. We find ourselves in circumstances where we could just make a choice to scratch that base human itch and play out a fantasy, satisfy ourselves. She will never know. It is impossible for her to find out. I am alone, in another city. No one knows me here. I can just do this thing, satisfy me and no one will ever be the wiser. No one will get hurt. It's just me.

Dangerous ground, my friend. Dangerous ground. The analogies run rampant. The tip of the iceberg. The crack in the dyke. The leading edge of the wedge that can open up an emotional abyss between you and your wife that you may never be able to bridge. You have got to ask yourself, "Is it worth it?" Am I prepared to pay for this personal indulgence with my marriage and all of the relationships and life that is built on that one certain thing?

It cannot be. There is no single thing on this earth that is worth that price. So, I implore you, do not put yourself in a position where you will be tempted to make the wrong decision. You know your own weaknesses. You know where you are vulnerable. You may try to hide it from everyone else, but you cannot hide it from yourself. You know exactly what kind of situation you could find yourself in that would create a temptation for you to choose a path that does not first honor your wife. Choose to avoid those circumstances.

When you are on a diet, trying to shed a few pounds, it is definitely easier to stick to the diet if you do not have all of your favorite treats stocked up in the cupboards. I just want to shed a few pounds, so that summer barbeque sized bag of cheese doodles and fudge cookies is no problem. I'll just nibble at them. Bonk! Doesn't work, does it? Empty your house of your temptations, fill it will healthy food and you maximize the opportunity to succeed in your weight loss. No one can expect to be successful with a diet if the fridge and cupboards are still full of cookies and cakes. Get rid of the temptation.

Similarly with your wedding vows, purge your life of the temptations that would cause you to make decisions that are not consistent with your promise to your bride. Just get rid of them, whatever they may be. In some cases, this may even entail letting go of some things that you hold dear, including friendships. If that is the case, then do it. All of it is secondary and if it cannot be a positive contribution to your marriage, it has no place in your life.

Like your promise to love your wife, to honor your wife requires action. It, too, is a verb. It requires specific behavior. It requires decisions when you are standing right beside her, when you are with others and apart from her and, perhaps, the biggest test, when you are alone and you think no one is watching.

Honoring your marriage can be a real challenge in the regular flow of your every day. Think about all the opportunities we have to step outside the boundaries of that honorable behavior. The obvious ones include what you are looking at on the internet when you are alone, flirting with that good looking woman at the office, going out for a drink with your buddies after work and slipping your wedding ring off your finger and into your pocket, just in case you happen to meet someone in the bar who might be fun to spend some time with.

The simplest analysis says all of that is just nonsense. You just have to give yourself a shake and say "This is stupid. I am not doing this anymore." And then, just stop even venturing down that road for any distance, for any reason. Just avoid it. You may not even be aware that you do this or that there is anything wrong with any of this because it is just the way you are and it is all harmless anyway. It is not that you would actually ever do anything with that good looking woman at the office or that young girl you meet at the bar. It's just all meaningless fun. Right?

WRONG! It is not harmless. It is not meaningless. Ask yourself this question. "Would I do this if my wife was standing right beside me, holding my hand?" If the answer is "no", then you shouldn't do it when she is not with you. It is that easy. You can ask yourself that and answer it immediately. Eventually, if you stay true to this test, the need to ask yourself the question will diminish because the circumstances that cause you to ask it become less and less frequent. Why? Because you will not allow them to occur in your life. You will not allow yourself to wander into a position where such circumstances could occur. They are just outside of the path you are walking. Not to say you will not be tempted from time to time. We are all human and imperfect. You may even take that first erroneous step in the wrong direction, but your instinct to self correct will be sharper and quicker. And, the frequency of your missteps will diminish. Your strength to dispatch the temptations and dismiss them will increase. But be aware, they will never become a non-issue. Therefore, there is no letting up on your diligence. You have to keep your head in the game.

Now, there are others of us for which these temptations can be and are a real issue. Some behavior would be considered addictive and impossible to resist. I truly encourage anyone who is experiencing struggles of that magnitude to seek professional help. I know it is embarrassing and difficult to admit we need help. But, the higher priority must be the marriage. You must want to protect and preserve and grow your marriage and for that, in this case, the price for achieving that greater marriage is to admit you are weak and need to learn how to manage yourself.

The opportunity to honor your wife and your marriage arises every day in your life. When you have a chance to talk about your wife, you can either marginalize her or hold her up. It is a simple demonstration of respect that she may never know about, because she is not there. However, my bet is that it will come back to her in any number of ways. How you treat your wife when she is not with you will contribute to how she is treated by you and others when she is with you.

For instance, when I am talking about my wife, I say "my wife" or "my bride" or "Laura". I never refer to her as my life partner, significant other, spousal equivalent, ball and chain, old lady, "the wife", common-law-wife, "friend with benefits", mate, "She-Who-Must-Be-Obeyed", co-habitor, fiscal partner or any other idiotic pseudo-wife equivalent. I hate these half-baked terms. And I know "hate" is a strong word. I hate the word "hate", too. However, I am not trying to be subtle here. Laura is the most important person in my life. She is my wife. She also is my bride, my best friend, my sweetheart, my lover and my girlfriend. She is also the mother of our children and she represents the best part of me. Calling her anything other than these terms of honest love in any circumstance does not respect the life and relationship we share. It dishonors the most important relationship I have. I just couldn't do that.

I have a friend who has been married for just a couple of years. He is a great guy and I can already see that he and his wife make a great couple. They are one of those couples whom you just know are going to make it in the long haul. Not surprising, really. They come from good stock. His father is a good friend of mine, too. The father has been married for over thirty-five years and every time he talks about his wife, you can see and hear the love and respect he has for her and the importance of their marriage in his life.

The son has lived observing this strong model of a great marriage his whole life. It is like being the student in a class for advanced education in marriage taught and demonstrated by his parents on a daily basis.

In many ways, that is the same for me. I have been blessed with a lifelong demonstration of what a marriage commitment really means in the example given to me by my parents. That's not to say I agree with and mimic everything I have seen of my parents. However, a great deal of the foundation that I believe is right for a marriage relationship I learned from them. I have been lucky that way.

One thing I have learned is that honoring your wife happens whether she is there or not. How you talk about her is just one simple way to demonstrate that respect. So, when I heard my young newly wedded friend talk about "the wife" with the same tone as saying "the old ball and chain" I called him on it. I just stopped him right in the middle of his story and said, "Wait a minute. 'The wife!' Did you say 'the Wife'"?

"It's alright," he responded. "She doesn't mind. I call her that right in front of her."

The other guys in the room, all of whom had been married longer than him, burst out laughing and moaned over the magnitude of his naiveté.

"You call her that!" I said. "Like it's some kind of label or conclusion!"

"She doesn't mind," he insisted.

"Oh. She minds," I said. "She minds. She just hasn't let you know yet. Trust me. It doesn't matter what she says now, no woman wants to be called 'the wife'. She is 'my wife' or 'my bride' or 'my sweetheart' or you can call her by her name. But don't call her 'the wife'. That just is not on."

The next time my friend was telling a story a couple weeks later that involved his wife, when the time came, he looked right at me and emphasized the words "my wife" when he came to that point in the story. I just nodded and said, "That's right."

Love and honor your wife, my friend. That comes first! Every day. With every step and breath you take. It is the core fundamental requirement that will guide you in all of your decisions in your shared life. It will define your and her happiness and the quality of that one life. When you love and honor your wife you are building happiness for yourself.

I haven't touched upon the third word in the vows – obey. Not many of us say that anymore I think. Some suggest it is a throwback to a different time and not really relevant or appropriate for today's world. I don't agree with that. Even though it was not a part of our wedding vows, I would have no problem making this promise to my wife. When you think about it, promising to obey your spouse is not a scary proposition. It does not suggest a slavery type of relationship where you are promising to do whatever your wife may order you to do, regardless of the nature of the command. I do not think that is what is intended by the inclusion of the word in the traditional vows.

If you are one of those individuals who spoke the word "obey" as a part of your marriage vows, do not despair. There is a very positive and generous interpretation of this promise that, when it is given as a mutual promise between husband and wife, it really declares to the world that you will pay attention to each other. It goes to one of the principal points of this entire book.

Look it up in the dictionary. Among other meanings, the word "obey" means "to follow the guidance" of others. Both husband and wife need to be open to following the guidance of the other because throughout our life we are constantly sending out messages deliberately or subconsciously. These messages tell the world who we are, what we are, how we are and what we need. If I am obeying the guidance that my wife is providing about her needs, then I am paying attention to her and trying to fulfill those needs. It is a big part of just trying to make her life wonder-filled and happy. If I am paying attention and responding to what I am learning about her along the way, then I am constantly following her guidance. And she is doing the same for me.

That works for me. It works because it is not a one-sided affair. We are both working at the same thing. By focusing on this, we are constantly improving our life together, sharpening the other person with our expectations of commitment to the quality of the marriage and fulfilling our side of the bargain with our response, or ideally, our proactive actions to address the needs of the other.

The wedding vows are amazing. After twenty-five years, I realize those few words cover the full spectrum of experiences – challenges and victories – encountered along the way.

I guess if you promise to be your spouse's sunrise, when the big tough circumstances arise (and we all know they will), it is fair to say, "Wait a minute. I didn't sign up for this. I signed up for sunrises." When you commit to love and honor each other until death you do part and you live that, then a day without a sunrise is just another day to keep working, to keep loving, to keep honoring. You know the sun will return.

When I Got Married,
I Was Young and Stupid
– At Least I'm Not
Young Anymore!

"I require only three things of a man.
He must be handsome, ruthless and stupid."

-Dorothy Parker

There is no end to the opportunities to take a wrong turn. And I am not talking about finding your way through the labyrinth of roads in an unfamiliar city. I will strain the analogy a little more and suggest that navigating through the road map of your spouse's emotions, needs and wants is an impossibly complicated undertaking. You do not want to get caught going the wrong way on a one-way street. You do not want to get trapped in a traffic jam, or caught running a red light, speeding, double parked or stuck on the off ramp of marital bliss.

I am not even sure what that means, but I am guessing at least somewhere in that traffic lingo is a seed of truth and you are nodding with recognition that the feelings of anxiety associated with being lost in traffic are sometimes not that far from the emotions you can experience when you feel lost in your relationship.

That is pretty natural. We all get confused. We get frustrated when we try to "get it right" only to find out we are so far wrong, we can't even identify how we got so off course. It's just all of a sudden – WHAM! – you are way out there, far, far away from the "safe zone". And, you can get whiplash with the speed that you can find yourself on the wrong side of a whole lot of unhappy.

Let me tell you about a couple of experiences that I actually had with my wife over a period of months and years. Together, these experiences added up to one big learning curve. Progress along the curve was, at times, painfully slow for me. It was undoubtedly very frustrating for Laura as well. Here's what happened (more or less).

In the early years of our marriage there were times when things were not all happy, happy, happy. It's not that the marriage was ever on rocky ground. We loved each other. We wanted to be together. In many circumstances, however, that is not enough to satisfy a personal need or satiate an unacceptable or unwanted mood.

One of the biggest things for Laura to deal with was homesickness. It still is. Our newlywed home was a small apartment. I had already been living in the apartment for some time. So, in one sense, she was moving into *my* apartment. It was not "our home" yet. It certainly would become our home as would several other residences in a few different cities over the ensuing years. But, in the early months of our marriage, the apartment was not her home. She missed home. From time to time she still does. But today, the implications of feeling homesick are completely different than the overwhelming sense of loss and want that characterized her homesickness at that time.

I did not understand how big that was to her at the time. It was very big. Our marriage pulled her out of her childhood home – the only place she had ever called home. Immediately after our wedding we were off on a two week honeymoon and immediately after that, but for a brief return to her hometown to visit with parents and pack up her entire worldly belongings and our wedding gifts, we left for our new home two thousand miles away.

The shock of being displaced away from her home, her family, her house, her room, her friends, the entire rhythm of her life and dropped cold into a new city where she knew no one was a very big adjustment. Add to that the further adjustment of moving into my apartment with me after only seeing me for the five days immediately before our wedding after a fourteen month separation. Add further to that the reality two days after arriving in our new city, I went off to work, leaving my bride completely alone in this strange environment.

Not surprising, there were a lot of tears in these early days. Sometimes I would do something that would trigger the tears and I would jump into damage control mode, guessing wildly about what to do to make the tears end and my wife's smile return. My fix was action – any action – with the hope that something would turn the tide. I was shooting completely blind. Laura would cry. I would respond with something. I would apologize for the thing that appeared to trigger the crying. Somehow I would succeed in only causing the crying and anger to escalate. I would try something else. The response was all wrong. I would panic. Try anything. All I wanted was for Laura to be happy, but I was missing something. Laura would get frustrated with me because I would try to force a conversation about what was going on and try to coax her out of her sadness.

"Can't you just leave me alone," she would say. "And let me cry?"

"No," I would respond. "I can't."

I could not leave her alone. My natural reaction was to fix it. I had to dig and dig and dig and fix this thing. It was unbearable to see my wife in tears. I had to fix this right now. I would become a "twenty questions" machine. Is it this? Is it that? Is it them? Is it us? You? Me? Did I do something wrong? Did you? It was like a free association nightmare. I was just casting wildly to try and land on something I could get my teeth into and work a solution. That was my nature. I was a problem solver.

"Augh!" she would exclaim in frustration and turn and walk or run out of the room, looking for a corner in our tiny apartment where she could just be alone. Into the bedroom she would go and the door would slam behind her. A fraction of a second later I opened the door and followed her right into the bedroom. Laura would be pacing back and forth like she was trapped – like a wild animal pacing a too small zoo enclosure. She looked like she was just looking to get out. Get some space. Get away.

Sometimes in these moments I would get a little ticked off. Who knows why? I probably felt that she was being unreasonable, that her response to a specific circumstance seemed out of whack with my perception of the magnitude of the circumstance. I would follow Laura into the bedroom and keep talking. I was actually trying to "reason" her out of her tears. I would say stupid things like, "You should not be crying about this." Or "This is nothing to cry about." Or "Stop crying. It's not helping anything." Or "Aren't you over this yet? How long is this going to go on? I said I was sorry. What else am I supposed to do?"

Do you think that any of these contributions to the circumstance would help in any way to resolve the situation? I was literally trying to force the outcome that I wanted. I thought that by sheer logic I could drive Laura into a different frame of mind and emotion. I had no chance of being successful. But I did not know that. I was relentless.

Laura would ultimately offer something back to try and snap me out of my logic frenzy. "It's not about that," she would say (the "that" being whatever I was apologizing for). That always threw me. Well, if it's not about "that", then what is it about? Confusion is not a good place to be when trying to deal with a highly emotional situation. Clarity is the desired state of mind. Clarity eluded me completely. I was heavy in "failure to understand" combined with "action to fix". I had plenty of both, but together, they were a pretty useless combination that nevertheless drove me on!

Sometimes these emotional volleyballs would be shooting by me so fast I just could not keep up. "Just tell me what's wrong. What do you want me to do?" I would plead.

"You know," she would respond and then stop. Nothing more.

"No. I don't. That's why I am asking you."

Then came that look like, "You idiot. You do so know what you need to do. You are just pretending you don't know."

No. Really. I don't know. That's why I am asking. I really don't know. It doesn't matter how smart I look. It doesn't matter that I am well educated, that I have a complicated job with high intellectual demands, that as a part of my profession I have to decipher the matrix of human and business complexities. It doesn't matter if I am a brain surgeon, an engineer, a plumber, a waiter, an inventor, a butcher, a baker or psychologist. When I am faced with the mystery of understanding my wife's emotional turmoil, it is not possible for me to come up with the right reason for her unexpected (at least to me) sadness. It is not possible for me to come up with the right response that will cut through the sadness, avoid the escalation of distress and detour the entire circumstance onto the gentle, downhill, smooth, clear path to recovery and happiness. I am too stressed out to even think straight. Please don't expect me to be intuitive, compassionate, empathetic and brilliant right now. Just help me do the right thing for you. What do you want?!

After getting nowhere, Laura would finally say with disappointment in her voice, "Just leave me alone and let me cry." And so, feeling defeated and befuddled and crushed from that look of disappointment she could throw at me with laser accuracy, I would leave her alone. I would leave the room. Close the door. Quietly tell her, "OK. I am just going to go into the living room." And then I would leave her, go sit in the living room and wait… and wait… and wait… and begin to read a book or watch TV. I mean, after all, you just can't sit there waiting and doing nothing indefinitely. Eventually, I would just return to normal. I would turn the TV on. But, I would turn the volume down very low. Don't want her to think I am out here doing what a typical guy would do – move on, but, by playing the TV so low, I guess that is exactly what the message is.

Anyway, after some time, Laura would re-surface from the bedroom, still on the fringe of crying. Not fully cried out yet. Puffy eyes, soggy tissue clutched in hand and she would appear around the corner and look at me sitting on the couch watching TV and then hit me with a brand new look – the complete disbelief and "are you in trouble now buddy" look.

"You're watching TV?" she says. But what I hear is, "This is unbelievable. I can't believe you would do this and be so insensitive to me?"

"You said you wanted to be left alone," I offer weakly with a pleading in my voice that is meant to convey "I am only doing what you want me to do."

Then the questions came flying at me like razor sharp accusations of insensitivity. They came shooting at me way too fast for me to have any hope of keeping up. I am on the ropes in a late round of the match taking body blows with no defense left. I am just trying to survive to the bell at the end of the round and then have a chance to re-group.

"How long were you planning to leave me in there alone?"

"Uh?"

"Don't you care about me?"

"Uhhh?"

"Can't you see that I am really upset?"

"Uhhhh?"

"How can you just sit there and do nothing?"

"Uhhhhh?"

Notice how much better I got at responding as the questions kept coming at me. Brilliant! So what do I do? I fall back to what I think is a safe position. "You told me to leave you alone."

"I didn't mean for you to leave me 'ALONE' alone!"

"Uhhhhhhh?" Then she rolls her red eyes and heads back to the bedroom.

Now I have to follow her and get back in the battle. So, up off the couch I get and head back into the bedroom with Laura. I don't know how this is going to go, but I am in it until the end now. I am going in completely unarmed as well. I am just going to have to react to whatever comes at me. There has to be a way out of this and back onto relationship terra firma. Somewhere in my mind I am scrambling for the right next move. I am not even sure what the whole emotional turmoil is all about. Now, however, I am fixed on trying to understand when she says "leave me alone" she does not mean "leave me alone until I am finished being upset." There is some sort of time limit to the "leaving alone" request that is implied. I did not know that. I'm a guy. If I say, "leave me alone" I mean leave me alone. I do not mean leave me alone until you should inherently know that I do not want to be alone anymore and then come back at that time to be with me.

Whatever the reason, I am back in the bedroom with my emotionally distressed wife, trying to figure out how to get to the end of this emotional situation. The exact details of how the situation gets resolved are a little hazy for me. But, I do know that we ultimately talk the matter through and move on. It is resolved more because of my wife's willingness to work within my needs – and those needs are action oriented. In my view we just cannot let whatever the problem is go until we get past that tearful condition. We have to stay with it until we figure it out. So, we ultimately resolve the issue.

The very worst circumstance for me to deal with in our home is if Laura is unhappy for any reason. It is an unacceptable situation. If she is blue, it is agony for me. If she is angry, it is an emergency for me. If she is uncharacteristically quiet, it is dangerous for me. If she is distant, it is worrisome for me. But the worst, bar none, is if she is sad. That is unbearable for me. I have to fix that right away. I cannot settle down without turning that sadness around. I cannot sit back and let her work it out in her own good time. My approach is to attack! Like a crazed evangelical healer trying to exorcise the demon within her, I must relentlessly pursue the sadness until it has fled our home.

The next time Laura was upset I tried to talk her out of it. She told me to leave her alone. So, I did. In just a few minutes she was fine. Everything had returned to normal. BINGO! Now I knew what to do!

Round three – Laura crying, me not knowing exactly what to do –brought to mind the lessons learned from previous experiences. "Leave her alone," my inner voice said. "Leave her alone." So, I did. Right from the start, when Laura left the room in tears, I did not follow. I left her alone.

Wrong move. Very wrong. I had abandoned my wife in her turmoil and offered nothing for her. I did not even demonstrate interest in her distress. Not a surprise this did not go over too big with Laura. That time I had it all wrong again. I missed the boat by a mile because I did not appreciate that this circumstance was different than the other circumstances. The tears came from a totally different place and the nature of Laura's sadness required a different response.

My reaction was to defend my actions. I pointed out how in the past I had tried different ways to deal with her tears. I reminded her that in each case she pointed out how wrong my response to her emotions was. I listed my efforts to anticipate, read the situation, learn from my past errors and then I laid out the closing argument that justified my behavior this time and from which there could be no rebuttal. I had demonstrated how I had followed her lead. I did what she had asked me to do. I was following the rules she had established for dealing with her when she was sad. Therefore, any failure on her part to behave appropriately and get over her sadness in a timely way was on her shoulders, not mine. I had done what was expected of me.

Actually, I didn't say anything like that to her, but, in hindsight, I am sure that is what it sounded like, or at least, that is what would have been taken from my defense of myself. But, after all of my positioning of the rightness of my position, Laura was able to succinctly counter that with how completely wrong I was.

What she said was something like this. Very calmly, quietly and thoughtfully she said, "Instead of telling me you are doing everything right and I am doing everything wrong, when you see I am sad, why don't you just hug me, give me a kiss, tell me you love me and ask me what I would like from you?"

D'oh! Why didn't I think of that?

This is really important for a number of reasons. It is especially important because in a marriage there are many things that are certain to occur that are integral to normal, healthy human behavior and relationships. One of them is sadness. Sometimes, thankfully rarely, my wife gets sad. As a husband, I have to deal with this circumstance in a manner that has nothing to do with myself and everything to do with what Laura needs at that moment. In my experience, nothing says that what Laura needs this time is going to be the same as what she needed the last time or what she is going to need the next time. What I have learned is that to help Laura through her sad moments, I have to pay attention to her. I have to really listen, observe, check with her, respond and remember, at that moment, what I signed up for.

I can say that easily while I sit in the calm, blue glow of the light from my computer monitor. But, reality often does not reflect this. Just because "I know" does not mean "I always do."

If you are like me, sometimes you don't want a bunch of discussion. You just want to know what to do. Just cut to the chase please! The frustration and failure to read the situation correctly and get on the same wave length as your wife can be a mystery not unlike deciphering some ancient Sanskrit writing when no one gives you a Sanskrit to English dictionary. Good luck! Reality just doesn't work that way.

After twenty-five years together, my lack of clairvoyance still confounds me at two levels. Not only am I no better at reading Laura's mind now than I was a quarter of a century ago. (One could suggest I am just a slow learner.) It seems that my wife's expectation that I am capable of such mental deciphering in any number of circumstances remains faithfully intact. Both she and I are constantly surprised that; one, I cannot do this and, two; that she expects that I can.

Who set us up for this? Who put this seemingly unmovable, unaltered mind set in each of us? Why do we maintain that this should be so? Note we do not share these points of view. They are separate and completely at odds with each other. I cannot understand why Laura expects me to be able to read her mind in any circumstance. She cannot believe that I cannot. It is a guarantee for getting on each others nerves.

It's remarkable really. Both of us have changed so much over the years. We have learned from each other. We have learned about each other. We are very close and 99% of the time, we are in sync. That math tells me that out of 365 days a year, we are off side with each other only 3.65 days. Taking into account seven hours a day of sleep that leaves about 62.6 hours a year when we are out of sync. That sounds a bit high for us actually. I do not think we are angry with each other that much. But, it shows that we have got it pretty good. Even when we are separated and I am sitting in another hotel room hundreds of miles away from home, we are generally on the same page.

Those days when we are off step with each other are incredibly rare and feel very awkward. They are uncomfortable, painful in an odd sort of way. Anxious. Like you are walking on eggs shells and you don't know why. It's the kind of feeling that we want to get rid of as fast as possible, but, sometimes, we are just stuck, unable to shake it and unable to nail down why we are here or how we got here.

Fortunately for us, these conflicting views rarely cause us any grief. I think that is because we have invested so much time together, investing in our relationship that the happy rhythm of our relationship rarely pops off the rails. I also think that because of this, no matter how minor the cause, when our life is off balance, we both just want to get rid of that anxiety as quickly as possible. We want to figure it out, address the issue and get it behind us.

The kicker is this. It is inevitable that the very time Laura needs me to be most perceptive of her feelings is the very time when I am most likely not to be very accommodating. I don't know if it is some kind of cosmic practical joke. But, when I am tired, just home from being away too long and all I want to do is sit down and do nothing; that is the very moment when Laura needs me the most.

Sometimes I think, "NOT NOW! I just want to be left alone. I want to read the paper, veg in front of the TV, fall asleep doing nothing. But No-o-o-o-o-o-o. I have to be on the top of my game. I now have to deal with something that I just do not want to deal with." Sometimes I just want to say "Tell me what you want me to do and I'll do it." I think I have even tried that a couple times. It didn't go over so well.

You have to think about how whatever you say or do is going to be received. I may just want to jump to the finish line. But, unless Laura is ready to do the same, my desire just comes off as dismissive and uncaring. It's like I am telling her that I really don't care how she is feeling or why. Just tell me exactly what your desired outcome is and I'll go with that right now. It'll save us all kinds of time and I am not up for the long debate or analysis right now. Let's just get it done now. So, if you know where your finish line is, tell me and we are there. Done.

You know, that just doesn't work. No matter how many times you try. It is just a Band-Aid, not a real healing.

Don't get me wrong. It's not that I am not dedicated to the relationship. It is not that I am uninterested in what is going on. It is not that I do not care about why my wife is, at this moment, unhappy or out of sorts. I do care about all of that. I do not want any unpleasantness in our life. But sometimes I just don't really feel like dealing with anything like that. Sometimes I just want Laura to deal with it herself and leave me out of it. I also want her to deal with it quickly and be done with it quickly. So, sometimes, the Band-Aid looks real appealing to me.

There are times when Laura realizes that I am not into the debate or discussion and she accepts that and just goes with the Band-Aid as the solution for this moment. We, however,

can live with that from time to time because of the investment made in the marriage, knowing that it will not be the
default method of resolution of issues as a pattern in our
life. In that case, it is simply one of us caring more for the
other person's tolerance in the moment than for our own
personal need. It all works out in the big picture when there
is a shared trust and confidence in the overarching quality of
the relationship.

There is one big difference between Laura and I when it
comes to moments when we are at odds with each other.
I can "deal" with things really fast and put them behind me
and I am done with them. As soon as I have a handle on
something, I quickly adjust, adapt, mitigate, act, rationalize
and I am done. No baggage. No lingering emotional turmoil.
I am done. A friend of mine who is educated in this sort
of thing tells me I am only using half my brain – the linear
half.

Not Laura. She likes to analyze. Back up to the beginning.
Work through it. Think about it. Work through the emotion
of it. Talk about it. Agree on what we (or she or I) are going
to do or already have done about it, resolve it slowly, maybe
analyze it again from another angle, right from the beginning and finally, she will be done with it when we land on a
common, calming place. When she can say OK, we understand all of this, we know what went "wrong", we addressed
it, we have agreed that we have learned something from it
and how to avoid the same anxiety in the future and we still
love each other. Then she is done with it. At that point for her,
like me, there is no baggage or lingering issue. She is done,
done, done.

The difference is the linear thinking that I obviously demonstrate and the more complex three dimensional process of

thought and emotion that Laura goes through to deal with a situation. One is not better than the other. They are just different. I am told by others wiser than me that this is pretty typical. Men, generally, do not value the texture that the emotional piece adds to a relationship as much as women do. We stand fast in our linear thinking and declare, "I yam what I yam" – like Popeye. Women work through things like navigating through a spider web. It is way more complex. My mind hurts just trying to comprehend it.

I don't think this description of our differences it too surprising to most couples. Why should we be surprised that every human being is different and that we each have to go through our own personal processes to be fully resolved with an issue or dispute? It is not important that we get there differently. What is important is that we each appreciate that we will get there differently and that we are both prepared to work within the other person's natural tendencies and needs and help our partner in this one life be resolved with whatever the issue is.

So, Laura and I handle discord quite differently within ourselves. I have tried to describe the difference so that you can appreciate the Mars/Venus thing that happens in our relationship that I think is often experienced by couples. We are all different. Thank God for that. What is important for us is that we understand and respect this difference in ourselves. Because we understand that it exists and is not likely to ever change, we find ways to work within those differences to help each other through times of discord.

The fact that our moments of imbalance are rare and minor does not take away from the importance of dealing with whatever comes our way. If we cannot handle the minor things, we certainly could never constructively handle the bigger things as they come. And they do come. People can get locked in the different ways they perceive the world, receive information and emotional input and their different responses to those external influences and their differences become a barrier to the resolution of whatever is confronting them. We all have our natural tendencies. The more we understand our own and those of our spouse the more we will be able to handle moments like this constructively, positively, lovingly.

Twenty-five years later we still have to work through our differences. Just the other day my wife and I were disconnecting. She had planned a get-a-way weekend for us at a bed and breakfast cabin in the woods about an hour's drive from our home. She was very excited about it. Really looking forward to it.

I was not excited about it. Now don't get me wrong. It's not that I did not want to go. I just don't get excited about things in advance. I never have really. At least I don't remember the last time I was excited in advance of an anticipated trip of any kind. Maybe it's because I travel all the time with my work. I am constantly checking in and out of hotels. I have gone through so many airport scanners; I am on a first name basis with the entire airport security staff in at least three airports. So, when a weekend away is approaching, I am not thinking about it. I am not anticipating it or imagining all the wonderful moments we will share alone in a cabin in the woods.

Laura, on the other hand, gets very excited with the anticipation of travel. She loves it. She is planning what she will pack, how she will pack it and thinks about every little detail of how the weekend, in an ideal circumstance, will unfold. I am sure she even thinks about what the weather should be like for the weekend.

Me – I just get up; throw some stuff in my suitcase and go. Let's see, three days two nights, I'll need a couple changes of underwear, socks, an extra pair of jeans and a couple of shirts and a sweater. The toiletry kit is always ready to go. There. Packed and ready. Takes about four minutes. Let's go.

I always enjoy "just us" time with Laura. I love it. It's truly *the* favorite thing that we can do together. It is the best gift we can give to each other – Time. I don't really care what it is filled up with. We can figure that out on the fly. I just don't spend any time anticipating the trip. My attention turns to the trip when it is upon us. Not before. I've got too much other stuff going on to spend time thinking about it until it is here.

That's the same when I plan our travel get-a-ways. I spend the time planning and arranging, making all the necessary reservations. But, once planned, I input all the necessary details in my calendar and I file it away until it is time to go.

So, this particular weekend, Laura had booked this bed and breakfast for us. The weekend started with us going out to lunch on Friday afternoon. I took the afternoon off to get a jump on the weekend. After lunch, we made a stop at an arts supply store, picked up some canvases and paint and headed to our studio where we painted together for the afternoon.

Laura and I both paint. We enjoy it together. I have to admit, Laura is the real artist. I love it, but I am not particularly good at it. However, we love doing it together. It is just one shared interest that we have nurtured over the last several years that we will be able to enjoy together for the rest of our lives.

On this Friday afternoon we were painting at the studio and Laura had called the bed and breakfast a couple of times to confirm directions to get to the place. It was way out in the country, in the woods, and we wanted to make sure we knew where we were going. The proprietor of the B&B never called back. Odd, we thought. However, we did have some minimal directions from a friend and thought we would head out and find the place.

As it turned out, our friend's directions were perfect and we drove straight to the B&B. As we pulled into the driveway of the place, we stopped because a steel gate was pulled across the driveway and was chained. That was not a good omen.

Fortunately the chain was not locked. I lifted the chain off the gate, opened it and we drove in. We parked beside the main house which was situated overlooking a lake with large windows taking full advantage of the view. We could see into the house. It was in complete darkness. No one was home.

We walked around the house for a few minutes and ultimately, we only had one choice. We left. We started heading back to the city and Laura called the B&B one more time, left a message on their machine that we had been there and asked them to call us when they arrived home.

So, there we were, our romantic weekend a bust, out in the country, late on Friday evening, getting hungry and trying to figure out what we were going to do next. We were both disappointed, but it is fair to say that Laura was more disappointed. She had been looking forward to this weekend in a big way. When Laura is set on something and that something doesn't happen the way she wants, she gets disappointed. Often, tears flow. Hey she's an emotional woman. She cries at Canadian Tire commercials. She cries when she's happy.

She cries when she is surprised, sad, frightened, excited. You name it.

I was disappointed, but I decided right there that I was not going to be disappointed. I just let it roll off my back and thought, 'Hey, one less night in a foreign bed. Fine with me. Let's have some dinner, go to a movie and go home to our comfortable bedroom."

Laura didn't want to do that. She wanted to be in a hotel, out of the house for the weekend. That was the plan. I just didn't pick up on that, and I didn't get that she wanted it that much even when she suggested we just find another hotel and stay there for the night. I took her suggestion as nothing more than a bit of brainstorming. Like "here's one option." My option was let's go home.

After a quick dinner in a country restaurant that served everything from pizza to egg rolls, none of it particularly appetizing and everything came with gravy, we drove home in a snow storm, the conversation limited. When we got home, the real conversation began. We both could feel that things were off a little. The night had certainly not turned out the way either of us had wanted. But, we have been disappointed before when things did not work out. It's no big deal. We just sort something out and move on. That night was, however, different. The difference was that Laura was really disappointed and I was not. That's what it came down to.

When I look at it now, it seems that the fact that I was not as disappointed as Laura had everything to do with my reaction to the circumstances and that is what put us out of sync with each other. Laura had even given me a hint of what she wanted. She suggested we just find another hotel and stay out for the night. That is what she wanted. I just ignored that because I did not want to do that. I wanted to go home. But, that's not what Laura needed. I did not read that. I didn't have to even read her mind. She told me and I still didn't hear it.

I was tired. That's OK. We are entitled to be tired. It happens. But remember what I said at the beginning of this story. It seems that it is always when I am tired a situation arises when I need to be particularly aware of Laura's needs. It is in those times that we seem to be most vulnerable to miscommunication. That is when it seems we are likely to have a conflict. This circumstance was similar to many other times in our life where we were just missing the mark with each other and, from my point of view, I just did not want to deal with it. My preference in the moment was for Laura to just get over it.

She was not going to do that. That is not the way she is wired. I know that. I also know that there are countless times in our life that Laura does just get over it and I am never the wiser for it. I just blithely go on with the day never realizing that she has, for my sake, just let something go when she would rather take the time to work through it with me. So, this is a long way from a one way thing. We both have many opportunities to accommodate the other person's natural tendencies and then there are times when neither of us are really in the frame of mind that is ready to so easily accommodate the other person. Not for any reason or rationale other than that is just where we are at that moment. It may be a need for rest. It may be the accumulation of what has happened to us during the day. It may be that we got a great e-mail from a long lost friend and that has just lifted our spirit to be particularly generous with ourselves right now, so we can just let a lot more roll without getting negatively engaged in the situation. It may be that something else has happened that has put us in a frame of mind or frame of heart that allows us to be ready to respond generously to meet the other person's particular need right now. Who knows what the chain of circumstances may be that add up to our capacity for tolerance and compassion or our readiness for battle at any precise moment? Maybe it is an accumulation of similar circumstances that for whatever reason, you just have not caught on to what your wife needs and she has decided it is time to sit you down and clue you in for a change. (That kind of sounds like it could be me sometimes!) I have already admitted that I am in many ways a slow learner. Thankfully, Laura is a very patient teacher.

There we were, in our twenty-fifth year of marriage, again finding ourselves in a situation where we were just not communicating well with each other. The work never ends. We still can learn a little bit more about each other. Hopefully we will then recognize the personal need in the future, when (note I did not say "if") the circumstance arises again.

That is all it is ever about for us – working every day with every small circumstance to improve ourselves. By always focusing on the other person's happiness, we are aware to the circumstances when that person is not happy and, generally, we both want to find our way back to that sustaining happiness again, as quickly as possible.

By never giving up on the small circumstances, I think we have avoided the pitfalls of the BIG challenges. We know they are out there. We have been blessed in that, although we have faced many big issues in our life, we have not had any experiences that have been a real threat to the certainty of our relationship. I think that all goes to keeping our eyes on the ball. Not letting things get out of hand.

I made a promise to Laura a long time ago that her happiness was my priority. That still stands true today although there have been countless times in our life together that I have forgotten about that promise and started looking after myself, protecting myself and my turf too much. Inevitably, when I remembered my promise, and focused on that, everything else seemed to fall into place a lot easier.

Through all our trial and error Laura and I have learned from each other. For every story I can tell about my response to her moods, she can tell a hundred stories about learning how to put up with me. When husbands and wives care for each other, they carry each other through low periods of emotional turmoil. That is when we build up the strength, the real muscle power of our marriages.

There is no one right way to deal with emotional situations. Every situation has to be examined and addressed in its own way. There are, however, a number of basic fundamentals that seem to stand up as true, regardless of the circumstances.

First and foremost, in all circumstances, your wife must know that you love her. That seems pretty obvious. Telling your wife you love her should be easy. "Sweetheart, I love you." That didn't hurt too much. Did it? I know, lots of Hollywood movies cast the man as incapable of getting these syllables past his lips. Remember the movie *Ghost*? Patrick Swayze's character could only say "Ditto" in response to Demi Moore's "I love you". Give me a break! I think you can tell your wife you love her. Do it. Today! And mean it! If it feels uncomfortable, get over it. Just like anything else, the more you do it, the easier it gets. Do it today. Do it tomorrow. Do it the next day.

Second, show your wife you love her. This is the trickier part. What works for my wife may not work for yours. Not every woman likes seeing her image on the jumbo-tron at the football game with a big message that says, "You are HOT!" That can really crank some people the wrong way. (By the way,

Laura would love that!) Some women like actions. Some like spoken words. Some like things in writing (and by that I don't mean a legal document. I mean a nice card or note.) Some like public displays of affection. Some like private moments of caring. You have to figure out what best fits your wife's emotional needs and do that.

Thirdly, when your wife really needs you in times of emotional turmoil, you have to be 100% there for her. You must focus on her. Trying to understand and meeting her needs is your only priority. It does not matter what else is going on. It all falls away when she needs you. It may get frustrating. You may be tempted to get angry. Don't. You must be tolerant and patient and compassionate and selfless. You must stay with her and support her until whatever is causing the distress is dealt with. Do not guess or assume you know what is going on. Make sure that you do. Ask, but ask in a way that tells your wife that you are sincerely trying to care for her. Learn from your history with your wife, but do not carry your history around like baggage and pull it out to use as an excuse or, worse, as a weapon against your wife. There is no gain in that.

Do not be concerned about how much you are investing in this relationship or that it may feel very one sided right now. Trust me, it all comes back around and when the roles are reversed, she will be there for you.

And finally, love her. I know this is a repeat, but I like this one.

Twenty-five years into my marriage, I'd like to think I have learned something about what makes my wife tick. I'd like to think that I understand her better, but not entirely. The circumstances that may have caused distress in the past are, if not eliminated, at least diminished. As for the circumstances of the future that will cause distress and sadness, well, we will deal with them as they come. My wife knows that whatever comes our way, if she is unhappy, I will care for her and stay with her until we have sorted it out. I will never leave her alone to deal with her sadness in isolation. We are in it together and her happiness is my number one priority.

It is a lot of work – glorious work. Work worth doing. And the work never ends. What would be the fun of that?

I will never learn how to read Laura's mind. I don't think I need to. I think I will always be surprised by her and that is great. I always want to keep my senses alert to her needs. I want to recognize when her needs are not being addressed. I want to be willing to find the solution that gets us back to that place where we both feel the relationship is in sync and working.

What's great about this is that I know she is doing the same thing for me, every day. I just don't know how much she is doing it.

I am pretty sure it is way more than I think.

Do You Think He Came Out of a Box Like That?

"Why does a woman work ten years to change
a man's habits and then complain
that he's not the man she married?"

-Barbra Streisand

One of my bride's favorite responses to any comment offered by someone that is complimentary to my behavior as a husband is, "Do you think he came out of a box like that?" And you know what? She's right. The obvious answer to her rhetorical question is "No". I didn't come out of a box like this. It took tremendous dedication, patience, coaching, love, perseverance, forgiveness and patience (did I already say that?) – on the part of my wife.

Let's back up a bit. For four and a half years before we were married, I lived alone. I had left the protective cover of my family home and headed off to university. But for holiday weekends and breaks in the academic year, I never really lived under my parents' roof again. After graduating from university I headed off to Calgary, Alberta to begin my career. During this same time, Laura was attending university herself – a different university than the one I was attending.

During her university years, she continued to live at home. In fact, other than her summer adventure in Calgary in 1978, our wedding night was her first night away from the family home she had lived in her entire life. Until our wedding night Laura shared a bedroom with her three sisters.

All Laura knew was her family life. I, on the other hand, had comfortably slipped into a bachelor life style, doing what I wanted, pretty much any time I wanted. So, it should come as no surprise to you that my habits did not exactly change overnight once we returned from the honeymoon and settled into our brand new life together in a modest apartment, furnished with all my university furniture. And, it should also not be a surprise to you that not all of my habits and routines were fully appreciated by my new wife. Keep going with this and you can probably figure out that my new wife's reactions to my routines were not always perceived as "fair" or "reasonable" on my part. Guess what? We had some conflicts at the beginning that took some time to sort out.

I recall one such incident. I had become involved with a city men's basketball league during my first year in Calgary. As a single guy, signing up and heading off for twice weekly games and practices through the long winter months with a bunch of buddies was a totally normal decision. So in my mind, there was no issue with just signing up again for another year. A totally normal decision.

It was so normal that I not only did not bother discussing the decision to play in the basketball league the first winter after our summer wedding, I did not say anything about it at all until one night I came home from work, changed my clothes and then announced as I was heading out the door, "I'm off to play basketball" and headed for the door.

"Basketball!" Laura exclaimed. "What do you mean 'basketball'?"

"I'm going to play basketball with the team," I replied, satisfied that by repeating what I just said with only a slight change in grammar and the addition of a couple more words somehow made it all perfectly clear.

Then I noticed the distress in my wife's face for the first time. Actually, it wasn't the first time ever. It was just the first time that day. There had been several other moments of distress in the early days and weeks of our marriage for reasons not dissimilar to this. So, I was beginning to get better at recognizing the look. Again she said, "What do you mean basketball?"

I then told her about how I had signed up for the winter basketball league and immediately started to explain that I had done it the previous year and I was just doing it again. As I was saying this with a bit of a tone that suggested I was entitled to this and that I really didn't have to explain myself and that I am capable of making these simple decisions for myself and that I shouldn't have to clear every little thing with her, I knew I was wrong. But, I couldn't admit that right away. That would be caving in too fast. I have to stake out my territory here and make it clear that some things are sacred and somehow, playing a sport that I had never played prior to my inaugural participation on the team the previous winter was one of those things

The goofy thing was I was a lousy basketball player. Truly I was the worst. I have said it before and I will stand by it. I am the worst basketball player God ever created. I didn't even like the game that much. That fact, however, had no bearing on my right to play. Participation on the team was viewed by me not so much as a manly right and a great way to have fun with the guys. I was never one of those guys who needed a "guys' night out". I was on the team because in the early years of my career, my efforts to fit into the whole corporate world and do the right things included playing on this basketball team with three other senior members of my firm. It was their invitation that got me on the team in the first place. I guess they were desperate for more players because there were no try outs. I just had to show up and I was on the team.

Anyway, there I was defending my right to play on a team that I really didn't enjoy, playing a sport that I was lousy at, for all the wrong reasons. Notwithstanding all of that background, I was standing there, in front of my wife, declaring my desire and entitlement to do this without the need to discuss it with her at all.

Oh, did I mention that it cost money to play in this league – extra money that we did not really have with my entry level salary and my wife still looking for work.

Oh there is more. Did I mention that my wife was painfully homesick during the first year of our marriage? Even today, twenty-five years later, she still gets homesick. Fortunately not like she did when we were newlyweds, but that feeling still floats around every once in a while and we have to deal with it. I, on the other hand, never get homesick. Never did. I don't know why. I had a great home. Great family. Happy life. But, when it was time to move out, I was ready. It's always great to visit my family, but I really can't say that I ever feel homesick. But, Laura was homesick and leaving her alone in the apartment all day, six or seven days a week while I worked long hours trying to kick start my career did not help. Leaving her alone in our apartment in a city where she knew no one but me even longer while I went off to play basketball in an attempt to contribute to my kick started career certainly did not make it any better.

So, is that enough going on in a single moment? Let's see, the situational dynamic included:

- Committing myself to an extra-curricular activity that does not include my wife and that consumes a significant portion of my free time without even discussing it with her

- Spending money we could not afford to spend on a non-necessity without discussing it with my wife

- Ignoring my wife's needs for companionship when she is feeling lonely; and

- Taking the attitude that I am entitled to this and don't need to get her "permission".

So, what did I do? Well, isn't it obvious? I went to play basketball. Yes I did. I went to the basketball game.

A penny did drop in my mind, though. I came home from the basketball game and had a gut feeling that something was amiss. I look back at that experience and realize it was one of the first times the reality that I was a part of a marriage began to sink in. Even though I had spoken the vows, enjoyed the honeymoon, integrated Laura's stuff into my apartment and we had played husband and wife for a few months, converting my thinking and my decision making process from one of a bachelor to a husband had not really occurred. That was a much slower process and it really began that night.

So, when my wife asks, "Do you think he came out of a box like that?" she knows what she's talking about. That situation could not possibly occur today in our marriage. But twenty-five years ago, it happened – more than once. I don't want to talk about it. Let's just say that at the beginning I was a slow learner.

The good news is my wife was and is a patient teacher. I think I have become a better student over the years as well. Fortunately the basketball experience did not create any permanent scars. I did eventually pick up that it was a bone headed decision on my part and apologized. Laura did not go crazy on me and accepted my apology. We talked about it. She came to some of my games. I skipped a few practices. Half way through the season I just advised the team that I was too busy and had to hand in my jersey. I don't think anyone was too disappointed with my departure from the team. As I said, I am the worst basketball player God has ever created. I think all of my old team mates would agree with that.

The result of the experience is that I was one step closer to understanding the importance of including Laura in all decisions that affect us. I understood her a little better. I understood what it took to be married a little better. I am sure Laura learned something about me through all of that, but you would have to ask her what that was. It probably was that I had a surprising ability to make dumb decisions randomly and that she had to pay closer attention to me than she thought to guard against such unpredictable errors of judgment.

Now I have to tell a story about Laura. Although I may be the easier target with plenty of fodder to use as examples of marital evolution, Laura has her stuff, too. It just seems so ridiculous in hindsight that we ever had any concerns about the quirks of our individual personalities when we were first married. It should be no surprise to anyone that when you walk into a marriage, you likely carry with you at least a few of the routines and expectations of your previous life either living as a single person or as a part of a family. To expect some of those routines to continue after your exchange of vows is not a big stretch.

In the early weeks of our marriage, I was sitting at the dining room table one Saturday morning, polishing my shoes. Laura came into the room with a pair of her knee high leather boots, dropped them on the table and said, "Please polish these."

"What?" I responded.

"Polish them, please" she repeated as she turned away without a hint of anything out of the norm. She wasn't kidding. She really expected me to polish her shoes like it was my job to do it! I, of course, did not register the "please" part of the request. I just immediately "heard" my wife order me to shine her boots.

"Really," I said. "I don't think so. If you want your boots shined, go ahead and shine them yourself."

Laura looked at me with complete shock. She could not believe I wasn't going to shine her boots. "But, it's Saturday morning!" she offered as a complete and compelling argument for why I should be shining her boots.

"So what!"

"So on Saturday morning the husband shines everybody's shoes."

"What!"

"That's what always happens."

"What!"

We obviously were not on the same page and the conversation was not getting us any closer. "What are you talking about?" I asked. "I don't remember anything in the wedding vows that sounded anything like 'love, honor and shine your shoes!'"

Laura's face changed instantly. She was confused. As we explored the misunderstanding, we discovered that every Saturday morning everyone in her family would drop their shoes on the dining room table and her father would shine them. That's just what he did. Maybe it was some ritual to ensure the children all had shiny shoes for church on Sunday morning. I don't know. We did not get that far. However, the Saturday morning Daddy shoe shine fest was a weekly part for her entire life. Laura made the simple assumption that this life-long weekly routine would simply extend into her married life and that I, the new "man of the house" would pick up right where her father left off.

WRONG! There was no way I was going to buy into this little habit. I stood my ground. I would do a lot for my bride. I would do anything for her. In fact, I would shine her shoes if she asked me. No big deal. It was the automatic expectation that I objected to. What rubbed me the wrong way was the assumption that I would just do this without the courtesy of posing it as a request which, by the mere asking, implies I also have the right to say, "No."

The result? I shined her shoes that day. And, I have shined her shoes every time she has asked me. But, I do not shine shoes every Saturday morning. That little family tradition may still continue in her father's home, but it did not gain any traction with me. If you want your shoes shined, you know where we keep the polish. Have at it.

Saturday morning shoe shines are a small thing. And the specific circumstances are not the point. What is the point is that in both of the circumstances – the basketball and the shoe shining – Laura and I each assumed that we were individually entitled to something without thinking about the other. Each of these circumstances related to small matters. I mean, really, who cares about either one of these. They were, fortunately for us, of little consequence themselves, but both provided us a great opportunity to examine and test what it means to be married.

We each discovered that we needed to adjust our pre-marriage thinking and move along in the "we are one" thinking and behavior. The things that I did as a matter of routine when I was single had to be re-evaluated in the context of this shared life. Little things like working ridiculous hours seven days a week without a hint of an explanation to anyone (read "Laura") or going out for a drink with co-workers after work with no concern for time or heading off for a run five minutes after I arrived home without any acknowledgement or concern that someone else (a.k.a. Laura) had spent the entire day alone and lonely and homesick, yet had put on a brave face and cooked a beautiful dinner for me or. Little stuff, you know.

OK. I did all of these, and more, all in the first few months of our marriage. I was definitely not in the habit of coordinating my life with another person. I have heard some men bristle at their wives' expectations that they "report in" or "get clearance from headquarters". It is always mentioned with the attitude of annoyance like coordinating your single life with one person who promised to share that same life with you is somehow a completely unreasonable expectation – a real "cramp my style" kind of inconvenience. So, what do many men do? They ignore it. After all, the proper order of life and the unspoken hierarchy of relationships is the guy gets to do what he wants and the piece of his life that is entangled with "the wife" just has to fit around that.

I hope that as you read that last sentence you thought, "That sounds ridiculous." I have tried to write it with just the right amount of "ridiculous" in it for you to land at that conclusion. However, the truth is – and I have seen it all too often – that this is exactly what happens, although the behavior may be rationalized away and the hard selfish edges smoothed down by the mental gymnastics of "guy reasoning". So, here's a tip for you. If somewhere deep in your guy-ness there is a sense, however fleeting, that what you are doing is in any way self indulgent, self centered, self absorbing, self satisfying, or any other "self-ish" kind of thing you can think of, it probably is.

Not only that, if you have a spark of this feeling inside you, no matter how quickly you can overcome it and charge on with what you want to do, it is likely much bigger than you think and there is someone else in your life who is experiencing the other side of that feeling. She is experiencing the ripple effect of your behavior. Her side of the feeling is loneliness, being ignored, taken for granted, not valued, un-loved, lack of respect and sadness.

Doesn't that sound like a recipe for happy! Can it be any surprise that your wife is not jumping for joy with the prospect of responding or anticipating your needs (e.g. food, sex) and does not put your desires up high on her list of priorities?

There is more to this. I am just scratching the surface. My point here is this. It doesn't matter how small the specific event or decision is. It does not matter how infrequent. It does not matter that your wife never complains or tells you she is hurt by this. It does not matter that your wife may not even recognize that she is hurt immediately. The truth is your behavior and the feelings experienced by your wife are cumulative. Ignoring them only goes to reinforce the behavior. Soon, you've got a pattern of self indulgence and hurt that neither of you can understand fully. Years can go by and you may never discover that you are just going through the motions. Each of you has found a way to ultimately get as much satisfaction out of your parallel lives and that satisfaction is not in any meaningful way (if at all) dependant on the other. She has her friends, clubs, work and volunteer activities. You have your old timers' hockey, work and internet porn. How does that sound? Do you think I am straining the logic just a little too much and that this is unrealistic? Or, does it sound just too much like your life?

How many marriages are into their second, third or even fourth decade and the couple are wondering what they are doing together? Well, my view is that it is never too late. However, you have to invest in the turn around. You have to invest in the smallest of things. Depending on the degree of dysfunction that exists in the marriage, the return on the investment may be slow in coming. But, just like compound interest on a long term investment, the payoffs accelerate as time goes on. You just have to have the patience to stay with the strategy and wait for it.

So, I have painted a rather bleak picture of marriages gone wrong where the joy of life has been drained out of them. I have described a path, or perhaps separate paths, trod by husband and wife after the vows have been exchanged that finds them a long way from the day they wrapped themselves in wedding lace and rented tuxedo and stood before a preacher. If you have been following, I have suggested this divergence of paths can all stem from failing to communicate in the early weeks and months of a new marriage on the simplest of things like participation on a community league basketball team or shining boots on Saturday morning.

I cannot possibly express how happy I am that a light went on for me in the early days and months of our marriage. I don't know why I clued in that I had to change my single ways. I made a mistake when I chose to sign up for basketball without ever considering my wife's feelings. Signing up for basketball was not the mistake. The manner in which I made the decision to sign up for basketball was the mistake. Fortunately, we found a will to work together to understand and learn from our early experiences as husband and wife and we have been building upon those early successes ever since.

I think the big wins in a marriage are built on the little things. I believe if we pay attention to the little things, when we are confronted with the big challenges in life, we will be well equipped as a couple to handle them and that from those challenges we will emerge stronger together than we were when first faced with a mountain to climb. That is why I believe it is so important to focus on the ordinary, everyday things. Those are the dynamics of life that we are all faced with everyday.

There are big things in life that I am not equipped to even discuss. I have never had to deal with addiction, physical, mental or emotional abuse, severe mental illness or psychotic behavior, violence or anything of such a magnitude as brutally difficult as these. My heart breaks for people suffering with these sad realities. I encourage you to seek out the very best professional help you can to survive and overcome these burdens. Take care of yourself. Protect yourself. Make decisions and choices that will lead you out of your troubles. Rely on friends. I pray that you find comfort and peace and healing in your life. Some marriages just cannot survive these or similar problems. I know this. I do not have the expertise to even contemplate offering comment or advice to those who suffer in this way. I will not even try.

I am speaking to those couples who live everyday with the ordinary life experience and who have within their grasp the ability to achieve the extraordinary in the one relationship that should matter the most to them – their oneness with their spouse. I am begging you. Do what you have to do. Get in the game. Pay attention. You have an amazing capacity to change your marriage for the better. And, once you begin to experience the momentum, you will never want to look back.

Here's how you get in the game. I just said it. Pay attention. That, in a nut shell, is it. Pay attention and act. If you really think about it, you probably already know what to do, but some "guy thing" is keeping you from doing it. You know your wife. You know what she wants. Give it to her. Give it to her every day without rest. If you really do not know what she wants, and I guess that is possible because you never asked or you haven't been paying attention, then start to pay attention or ask. How hard is that? I know. I know. It runs against your natural tendency to never ask for directions because it's a sign of weakness. But, you know it really doesn't hurt that much and if you put it together correctly, the simple act of asking your wife what she wants may just give you a surprising and favorable response. A little sincere vulnerability can go a long way. It doesn't make you a milk toast. What kind of woman wants a milk toast any way? (Actually, I am not sure what "milk toast" means, but to me, a piece of bread soaked in milk is pretty pathetic, limp and weak. Who wants to be that?)

I think women want real men to be men. Some guys think a real man is this hard attitude, ask no questions, take no prisoners, gun rack, deer antler truck decorated, beer swigging, bar fighting, (add your own cliché) kind of guy, regardless of whether you are working the back forty or making the big deals in your designer suits on Wall Street. Ask a woman what she thinks a real man is and see if any of these descriptions come up. I'm guessing they won't.

I am also not suggesting that you have to become a love poem writing, flower buying, gourmet cooking, romantic love machine (although a little romance wouldn't hurt). Some guys just are not the romantic type. Some women are not either; although, I think that is less rare. Have you ever seen a woman respond to a story about romance with a shrug or an exclamation like, "Well that sucks!" or "What a waste of time." I can't say that I have. I have seen, on the very rare occasion women uncomfortable with a display of romance, but not a rejection of it. And generally I interpret that as a defense mechanism on her part to quickly rationalize the romance away because, quite frankly, that's the only way she can manage the lack of romance in her own life. My experience is when a woman or a group of women hear a romantic story or witness romantic behavior, their response is virtually universal. It's that recognizable daytime talk show audience "Ahhhhhhhhh" sigh that you hear which says in all languages that she approves.

Most of us do find someone who is reasonably compatible with us. It is the erosion of that compatibility that occurs over time by ignoring, or worse, being indifferent to, the needs of the other person that eventually breaks the relationship down. That, my friend, is what we have to avoid. It can happen so easily, so effortlessly. We can live our lives blithely unaware that we are wasting the very best part of our life.

We just sleepwalk right through it. By the time we wake up, it may be too late.

Those of us at the beginning of our marriage relationship or perhaps contemplating marriage need to prevent that erosion. Those of us who are into our marriage need to stop further erosion (assuming we have caused some already) and build the relationship and the compatibility, back up. We have to shake off our indifference and care!

I have already stated how to do it. But, like any other advice book I have ever seen, the way you fill the pages of a book is to repeat the same thing over and over again and pepper the repetition with stories and examples. Repeat it enough times and you have a book!

Here's what you do. It only takes two steps. Real easy. You ready?

Step 1: Pay Attention

Step 2: Take Action

How easy is that? I could make it even easier. I could replace Step 1 with "listen". Then it's down to only two words – listen and act. OK. Go. I have given you the untold secrets of the universal truth for an extraordinary marriage. Go. Be extraordinary. No thanks required. I thank you for accepting this profound pearl of wisdom that has been kept tucked away and hidden for millennia. It was only through my Indiana Jones-type escapade into the darkest unknowns of lost history, battling undercover villains and counter-terrorist forces, with my life threatened by disease and skullduggery that I was able to unearth this long lost secret of the ages. Now it is out there for the world to consume at its pleasure. Go now armed with the truth and be extraordinary.

OK. Maybe it's not that easy. I know so many guys who are great guys. They are loving men. They love their wives. They care about their wives. They want to be happy. They want their wives to be happy. But somehow, there is something that just prevents them from getting to that point of understanding and giving that addresses a need that is left unfed.

There is a lot to these two words – listen and act. I am making it sound easy. It is not. It is incredibly challenging. We have to give this daunting task the respect it deserves. After all, it summarizes the efforts of an entire married life. Let me explore it just a little bit more with you. I'll never get to all of it. I don't know enough about it really to get to all of it. I am sure there are entire books written about each of these actions. There has to be. I just want to give you a few ideas and examples about what I mean when I say "pay attention" and "act".

Early in our relationship I would not have been considered a romantic guy. In retrospect, I think I had it in me because I think I have become romantic over time. But, initially I was a bit of a dunce in that category. For example, our first Valentine's Day together I just ignored – completely. There was no card, no flowers, no chocolate, no acknowledgement of any kind that Laura was special to me. I was of the view that Valentine's Day was just another excuse to spend money. It was a fabrication of the card manufacturers and retailers and florists of the world. I was not going to have any part of that commercial brainwashing. So, I did nothing.

Laura, on the other hand, thought Valentine's Day was a brilliant opportunity to let that one very special person in your life know that he or she is special. So, she did. She celebrated her love for me with the appropriate recognition. She gave me a card and a gift. I opened them both and thanked her. But, I had nothing to give her in return.

I gave her the whole commercialization argument as a reason for my lack of consideration for her, but I knew I could not talk myself out of it. I failed to realize how important it was for Laura that I demonstrate to her that I loved her. I felt like such an idiot.

I learned. The very next year and every year since, I have been on the ball with a gift and a private celebration of our love for each other. The celebrations have varied over the years. What we do or the gifts we exchange on Valentine's Day really are not important. What is important is that we take the time to celebrate being together and love each other, especially on that day.

I have not worked on Valentine's Day in twenty years or more. It is a day reserved for just us. Laura protects that day for just us, too. That, alone, is the best gift of all.

Here is another example of how I have changed thanks to the influence of my wife gently guiding me along the way. My proposal of marriage to Laura was a complete and utter disaster. I did not have an ounce of romance in me. I did not really think it through. I made no plan to ensure the mood and the atmosphere was just right. I did not create or seek out a romantic staging for when I popped the question. I have since heard and witnessed so many wonderful ways that guys have been really creative when asking their girlfriends to marry them. Every time I think, "Why didn't I do something like that?"

None of that nonsense for me. No sir. Who needs romance when you've got cake! That's right – cake! Laura and I had dinner at a steak house in our home town on the day I proposed to her. It was her birthday. I was nervous all through dinner, but I was determined to "get it over with" sometime during the meal. That is right. I said, "get it over with." That is really how I felt. I just felt I had to get this question out. I knew she would say "yes". At least I was pretty sure she would say "yes". I just had to get the question out there.

During our dinner, one of Laura's closest friends, Barb, showed up at the restaurant with another friend in a gorilla costume. Don't ask me why. I don't know. Barb just thought it would be hilarious to show up with a gorilla in the restaurant for her friend's birthday. Perfect. Just what I needed – competition for the most original birthday gift idea. I thought a diamond ring and a proposal of marriage would be a pretty good birthday surprise. However, now I had to wait for the opening act to finish.

But they didn't finish. Oh no! They sat down and joined us for dinner! Perfect! Just what I wanted!

Finally, Barb and the gorilla left. We wrapped up the left-over birthday cake and headed to the parking lot. My heart was racing. The meal was over and I had not accomplished the one single thing I wanted to do at dinner. We were still not engaged. As we approached my Dad's pickup, I opened the passenger door and placed the left over cake on the seat of the truck. On the way to the truck I had managed to re-trieve the ring from my pocket and I had it in the same hand that was holding the cake box. I placed the cake box down, wheeled around in a panic and thrust my arm straight out toward Laura's face, the ring pinched between my thumb and forefinger. I just stood there. I did not say a thing.

Laura looked at the ring, then the cake, then at me, then the cake, then the ring again and said, "Did you pull that out of the cake?" I just stood there staring at her, my heart pounding a thousand beats a minute. She looked at me again and said, "Well, aren't you going to ask me?"

I finally found my voice and I did ask her and she said, "yes".

Not very romantic. But, it got the job done. That is a pretty good summary of how I handled romance in my youth. Not very romantic, but I got the job done. In other words, I was atrocious. Yet, somehow I managed to convince a very romantic woman to marry me. I guess I showed some potential. I certainly have learned lots from Laura over the years simply by watching and listening and paying attention to her. She has shown me what she wants and needs and I have tried to respond to the messages that she continues to send to me. Her words and her actions have guided me and helped me to be a better husband for her.

Laura likes romance. I need to pay attention to that and create romance for her because it makes her happy. I need no better reason than that. Fortunately, now I like romance too. When I think of that first Valentine's Day and my marriage proposal to my wife, I wish I could have those moments over. I would do them so much better now. But, they do make good stories.

There is so much communication going on all the time between you and your wife. It's a constant stream of messages, some conscious and a lot subconscious. Or, perhaps it is deliberate on the part of your wife and you are just not picking up on it. Or you are picking up on it, but you cannot interpret it. So, rather than taking the time to figure it out, you just get past it by ignoring it or just wait it out until the momentum of the day pushes you past the specific feeling or moment.

Well, you should not let the moment go. You are "hearing" something. So listen to it. Find out what is going on in your wife's mind and heart. If you are not used to reading the situation, do not guess. Just ask her. I think the best way to get to it is to admit you just don't know what is going on. Of course you have to use a little sensitivity going in. You know your wife well enough to know what kind of comment will be useful and constructive and what you can say to basically shut down any hope of getting to whatever is going on in her mind. And don't say you don't know. You do. You may just not want to admit it because it is an easy excuse for not paying attention. "I just don't get my wife. I'm not a mind reader." Well none of us are, buddy, but many of us don't use our lack of Kreskin-esque skills as a reason for not communicating with our wives.

What's wrong with this? "Sweetheart, this is what I am sensing. I feel like there is something going on that is bothering you. I just don't know what it is and I cannot figure it out. I just feel that I am missing something or misunderstanding something that may be important to you and I want to understand it. And I want to know if there is anything I can do for you." With this, you are asking your wife for help. You are asking her to help you understand her better. There may be no magic turn around immediately. You may not get to "it" right away. It may take days or weeks or longer depending on the patterns of your relationship that you have created and breaking those patterns may be a bigger job than a one-time attempt. My advice is stick with it. Remember your steady investment in turning this established dynamic of non-communication around is the compound interest in the long term commitment of and to your relationship. When it starts building on itself, the return on your investment just takes off.

The art of communication is understanding your audience (in this case, your wife) and working within what works for her. I'll save expansion of this idea for later. Does it not seem like the epitome of idiocy to expect your wife to communicate with you exactly as you would like it yet not even consider what might work for her? Just standing barking at each other (I don't mean literal barking, I mean just talking at each other) in a manner that makes perfect sense from your point of view without trying to understand and interpret what is trying to be communicated to you is a marital Tower of Babel. No one is going to understand anything. It will just all be noise, likely unpleasant noise, and lead to unhappy outcomes.

A truly great marriage takes time. It takes effort. It takes two people who are willing to learn from and to teach each other. Does this sound earth shattering to you? I doubt it. This is not "rocket surgery" (to quote a Canadian Hockey Icon). The challenge seems to be in translating this simple truth into practical daily behavior. Every day there is an opportunity to learn from each other. Without exception. Some days the learning can be big. "I never knew that when I refer to you as "the wife" that is hurts you." Some days it may be just confirming or reminding you of what you already know, but with a slightly different twist. "I know your pet peeve is scraping left over butter back into the butter dish, but I didn't know it also included scraping left over jam back into the jam jar." (p.s. that's one of my pet peeves. It drives me nuts! Why not just spit in the jam jar right in front of me and call it a day!)

The reality is I am a much better man today than I was when I started this adventure twenty-five years ago. I am not the same person I was when I got married. It's not like I have gone through a personality change. I am, fundamentally the same person, aged and matured, older and wiser. I would like to think that my strengths are stronger and my weakness tempered with awareness.

And my wife is right. I did not come out of a box like this. I have evolved. I have learned. I have been open to discovering how I could be a better husband. It has not always been easy. I have resisted change on more than one occasion – on many occasions actually. Nobody likes to change. Generally, unless we are full of self loathing or some other self destructive psychological issue, we are pretty happy with ourselves. We all think we are funny and witty. We believe we are relatively good looking. We convince ourselves we are appealing to the opposite sex and some of us exist in the delusion that we are, in fact, irresistible.

No wonder we do not want to change. But, we have to be open to it. We have to believe that there is room for improvement. Once we take that leap, the change itself is easier. And once we have success with experiencing the positive outcomes of change, we are encouraged to continue along the path of improvement. Makes sense, doesn't it? Do something, receive positive feedback. That makes you feel good. Feeling good makes you want to repeat the behavior.

So, I did not fall out of a box like this. I have made every mistake in the book. Well, maybe not every mistake, but I have made a pile of them. I have learned from them. We have worked together to face every challenge that has come upon us as husband and wife and we have taken the time to pay attention to each other and to act in a manner that considers what is most important for the marriage. And we have survived. Our marriage has more than survived. It has grown and fulfilled us in ways not imaginable when we were young newlyweds, barely old enough to vote, exchanging vows before our family and friends.

So, I take the position that I did come out of a box like this. Well, at least I had all my parts, but… some assembly is required.

I Get Everything I Want

"I have learned that only two things
are necessary to keep one's wife happy.
First, let her think she's having her own way.
And second, let her have it."

-Lyndon B. Johnson

I get everything I want in my marriage. It's true. I always get my way. Does that sound fishy? Yes, it does. Even to me. Sometimes I don't feel like I am getting my way. Sometimes I feel like I am getting burned. Whenever I feel that way, if I take a breath and really see what is going on, inevitably the feeling is me just being selfish. Sometimes I get it. Sometimes I don't. Laura is incredibly accommodating of my selfishness when it shows up. When I rise above those all too human emotions of self interest, stand back and look at the whole picture, I really do get my way all the time. I can say that because of what I am about to tell you.

The wedding vows are a powerful thing. They forever shape your frame of reference for your entire life. At least they should. If seriously taken to heart, they will impact all of your decisions from that moment forward. That is not to say that you will always make the right decisions. We all fall short.

Too many times to count. But, the commitment to pursue achievement of those vows throughout your life will constantly right your course.

I have so often heard people talk about the sacrifices made for the sake of the marriage. Just think of the examples where this concept has been used to explain some circumstance. Her career never really developed the way it could because she had to sacrifice her opportunities for the sake of the marriage. He never realized his desire to start his own business because he had to stick to the safe cash flow job for the sake of the marriage. We sacrificed this thing or that activity for the sake of the marriage.

All this "glass half empty" point of view literally blames the marriage for all the "coulda, shoulda woulda's" of our life and sets us up for being disappointed at some level because we got married. That's nuts! Why hang on to such a negative spin. It is bound to pop its ugly head up sometime in your life, probably many times, and try to drive a wedge between you and your wife for some misconstrued opportunity lost because of the marriage. It is the marriage's fault for this thing that I do not like in my life. But, I'll take it because it is a sacrifice I am prepared to make... for the sake of the marriage. Sometimes, the decision is that you will not "take the hit" for the sake of the marriage and the marriage suffers, or worse, ends.

I just do not feel that way about any of the choices we have made in our life. I honestly believe and hold the view that I have not sacrificed anything in my life for the sake of our marriage. Sacrifice implies that I had a choice about something. I had options. The options varied with promises of different results, consequences and benefits. The option I really wanted was the best – for me. It promised me the most satisfaction personally, but, it would have taken away something from my marriage. So, I took my less favorable option because it did not have the same impact on my marriage, even though the marriage would have been just fine if I had gone with the one I really wanted. It would have survived. It's not like my real preference would have threatened divorce or anything. But, nevertheless, I sacrificed. I gave up my preference for the sake of the marriage. Now I have a little regret that I can hang on to and maybe pull out at some later time as an excuse for something else. Sacrifice implies regret.

I do not view options as sacrifice. They are choices. If you want, consider them as investment options. The point is that your attitude about selecting between options can make all the difference. Is it a choice or a sacrifice? Does it support what you really want, or is it a compromise with caveats?

I do not want to suggest that sacrifice is a bad thing. It certainly is not. I know many people who openly talk about sacrifices made for a more important goal or priority. When I talk about marriage with my own parents, and the subject comes up a lot more often than you would think, my folks often say that they sacrifice for their marriage. In fact, in some ways, their point of view, shared by many people I know, is that they have made lots of sacrifices along the way. But, for them, it is not a negative thing or a matter of regret. It is just doing what is necessary, what is expected, what is required for the marriage. From their point of view, sacrifice is just part of the deal and not a negative part. It's not a big deal. It just is what it is. That is not unhealthy. The unhealthy view is if the sacrifice, or choice, is seasoned with regret. That is what we must avoid.

The choices we all must make as a part of our married life can be significant. Think of the big issues that come along in a lifetime. Financial challenges, job opportunities, moving the family to another city or town, social activities, family commitments for children's activities, vacations, your choice of friends, what church, if any, you attend, involvement in community or voluntary organizations. The list goes on and on and many of the issues come back again and again and again. Every time there is a choice. Every time there can be a sacrifice. Every time you have a chance to invest in your marriage.

So, how do you do it? How do you make those choices? How do you confront all of this and filter through the distractions to find the way that will continually build your marriage? Again, it is called priorities. It's not a big secret. It is not even remarkable that I point this out. I am not sure if there is anything more obvious. But, I have been witness to circumstances that have resulted in a complete abandonment of the priority that the marriage comes first. The results were disastrous.

I have friends, Bob and Brenda (not their real names), who were married young. They met when they were in university and married in their early twenties. Both of them were dedicated to their marriage. They had four children. They were both well educated and for many years, Bob was the principal bread winner for the family. He pursued his professional career hard, long hours, long days and years, to try and build a successful business within his chosen profession. Brenda supported Bob consistently throughout this period of their marriage. She even worked part time in his business. They experienced many ups and downs along the financial roller coaster, but survived it all. Their four children were incredibly talented and gifted and intelligent and were given every opportunity to grow up in a nurturing environment.

As the children grew up and began to set off on their own roads of independence, Brenda began to chase a few of her own dreams. She became incredibly successful in her own right in a professional capacity. At the same time, Bob's career and business just took off. They became a real "power couple". They had survived the challenges of fiscal uncertainty and had safely achieved financial security and social standing.

Success breeds opportunity and both of their careers presented options for both of them that required the other to bend or "sacrifice" to allow the one to take advantage of his or her opportunity. It became a real bone of contention between them. Why should Brenda sacrifice? Didn't she give up her first career to stay home and raise the kids and support Bob in his business endeavors? She created this great career opportunity for herself after working her way back into the work world and she deserves this. It is her turn.

Why should Bob back down? Didn't he sacrifice everything to build his business to this point? Wasn't he the one who got them the big house in the classy part of town? The Mercedes? The vacation home in the mountains? The family trips to Europe? His efforts, his sacrifices got them to this life style that they enjoy. And now he has the opportunity to take his business to the next level. He can take it national and it is going to require him to spend a lot of time away from home, building the business in other centers across the country. The upside is huge. They are going to be very wealthy. But, to do it, Bob needs Brenda to back off of her career opportunity and be supportive of him.

So, what do they do? How do they choose? Who gives in? Who wins? Who loses? These are the very questions that too often couples face. There is going to be a winner and a loser.

That is what it boils down to. Someone is not going to get her or his way. And even the one who does "win" likely feels some regret in the victory. If not conscious recognition of it, the victory is certainly less satisfying than if the couple had reached a shared decision together.

If there is no feeling of regret – even a hint of it – then, over the long haul, that does not bode well for the couple either. Really, it says that the investment in the marriage is not there. Something is lacking. Without a change to that frame of mind, I think that the marriage is not likely to achieve the fulfillment that is promised at the beginning of the journey together. In that circumstance, the singleness of the person is still winning. That person has not invested his or her singleness completely in the marriage and therefore, the marriage cannot achieve the limitless possibilities of a true joining of two lives into one. The common ground is, in the long run, far more satisfying.

So my question is this. Why does there have to be a winner and a loser? Why is that the choice? I don't get it. We put so much pressure on ourselves to overachieve or risk that society will label us failures. We chase the greener grass on the other side of the fence. We acquire all the trappings of success that society tells us is important or we get wrapped up in the pursuit of that stuff. It's all nonsense, because we can lose track of what matters. We can lose track of what is truly important. When we do lose track, we greatly diminish our chance of making the right decisions when we need to. We lack the clarity of purpose to guide us in our decision making.

Success is a wicked temptation. Ego is never satiated. Professional recognition and position in society can come at a great cost.

What did Bob and Brenda choose? Well, I wish there was a happy ending to this story. They both chose their careers. And the price of that choice? A twenty-seven year marriage ended. How are they doing now? I really don't know. We have lost touch over the years, but a few years after their split up I ran into both of them on separate occasions and, in both cases, without any prompting from me, they both raised the subject of the loss. I specifically refer to it as a loss, well, because it was. But more to the point, each of them spoke of the terminated marriage as loss. Not very deep into each conversation, the feeling of regret came through in what they said and how they said it. There was a little too much bravado in Bob's declaration that he has a new woman in his life. Brenda was a little too quick to validate herself with her newest career initiative. Oddly, one of the career opportunities that had driven the wedge between them had evaporated away and she was starting all over with a new career initiative.

It is sad, really. We can so easily confuse professional success with personal success when really the latter is the only one that matters. My observation and experience is that if we focus on personal success, the other seems to fall into place quite nicely. Get them backwards and the odds of falling short on both dramatically increase.

It gets down to priorities, my friend. Most important is that the priorities are shared and agreed. The stronger your foundation, the more sustaining it will be. Two careers is a big wedge issue in a marriage. Or, it can be. But there are lots of such issues – extended family, friends, kids, money, faith, sexual appetite, stress. These can all end up driving a wedge between a husband and wife and without an agreed game plan to address these and thousands of other life issues, you and your wife will have real battles sorting out how to address the options as they come along.

It is so important to establish early in your relationship with your wife what your shared priorities are and will be. If you are already well into your marriage and you are reading this and realize that you do not have shared priorities, it is never too late. Get on it, now! I can promise you that when you and your wife are staring down a challenge, the whole situation is viewed differently if you are starting with a secure confidence in what you already sincerely agree to be important.

It can be a very difficult conversation. The whole concept of shared and agreed priorities only works if you are truly honest and clear with each other. Sincerity must prevail in this conversation, even if the conversation becomes a debate and the debate becomes an argument. It could be one of the best, most valuable arguments you ever have. It can literally save your marriage. If one of you just "agrees" for the sake of agreement, that behavior can become entrenched in the priority of one, but not shared by the other. Then you have got a mess and it is just a matter of time before it blows up in your face.

Shared priorities help sort out your options and narrow the choices. They help direct your actions and decisions and create an environment where the choice, once made, is accepted happily and without regret. The decision, whatever it may be, becomes the preferred choice and there is no sacrifice. It is all choice.

So, discuss with your wife what is most important to her and to you. Identify differences and shared values. Land on the core values of your shared life and hold on to them at all cost. They will serve you well over the long haul. Trust me on that. It seems so second nature to me, that to actually try to reduce this idea down to words is difficult. Perhaps another example may help.

It is not enough to have priorities. It is also important that they are clear. For Laura and me, our priorities have been clear from early on in our relationship – Our God, Our Marriage, Our Family. Everything else is a distant, distant consideration once we have considered all of these things. Even friends, as much as we love and cherish our friends, there is absolutely no doubt in our relationship that if a friendship became a threat or damaging to any of our priorities, both of us would make the choice that the friendship would have to be reconsidered. I would never want to say a friendship would have to end. That seems just too severe. Who can ever have too many friends? But, the truth is that if it came down to that, each of us would make that choice for the sake of our marriage.

I mentioned our first priority is our faith. Laura and I are both committed to and really enjoy our faith. We enjoy the peace and comfort and strength we draw from our personal relationship with Christ. That's our choice and it has never, ever, let us down. Our Christian beliefs frame our entire life. That probably comes through to you throughout this book without the need for me to be quoting scripture along the way. At least I hope it does. But, the ideas I share with you here are not reserved for the Christian man. They are true for every husband, regardless of your personal religious affiliation. For me, placing my relationship with God squarely first in my life helps me put everything else, even my relationship with Laura, in a clearer light and greatly helps me sort out the challenges along the way. It also helps me resolve the times I trip and fall, find a path back to what I know is right and recover from and learn from my mistakes. Hopefully, at the end of the day I can say notwithstanding my stumbles and falls, I have, overall, lived a life worth living, loved unending and shared the best of myself with the one person God gave me to share this worldly life with.

My friend, regardless of your personal religious convictions, you have to get on the same page as your wife. That's the "short and to the point" point of this chapter. You do that with clear priorities that you can agree on. Think about my friends with the competing career opportunities. They each had individual career opportunities. Neither one of them was prepared to invest their opportunity to advance their individual careers for the cause of their marriage. Note I did not say "sacrifice for" their marriage. No. What they had was a separate list of priorities and those two lists were not compatible. They survived twenty-seven years of marriage without ever realizing their priorities were not the same. And when the big challenge came, they had no way to resolve the conflict that allowed the marriage to win the day. So, the marriage was the currency used to chase the two diverging careers. Ironically, a few years later, the careers that were so important, or at least one of them, was gone and so was the marriage.

I know so many couples today struggle with this same issue. More marriages and families have to manage the reality that both husband and wife have careers outside the home. This is incredibly difficult to do well and I respect and admire those couples who manage to do this well for themselves and their families. It shows an amazing amount of commitment and dedication and focus.

Two careers in one marriage is probably one of the most difficult things to manage well within a marriage relationship. Everyone has to deal with it in some way. I say everyone purposely because even though I am talking about two careers outside the home, the truth is that there are always two careers going on within a marriage. One of those careers may be the one of homemaker. Some couples do choose to have one of the parents, most often the woman, stay home to raise children while the husband is the principal cash generator for the family. I know some families where these roles are reversed. In any case, both people are still fully employed in their respective roles.

In my view, the home maker career is as much a career as any other career. In our family, we decided that Laura would stay at home with the children and I would continue with my career. Over the years Laura has always become involved with some activities outside our home. She has worked as an actress, artist and singer and is incredibly talented in all of those areas. But, for our family, she has been wife and mom and has created a beautiful home and life for us. I call her the CEO of the family and that is absolutely the truth. She runs the family and without her, we would be a mess.

Laura's role as CEO of the family was a shared decision for us. To make that decision we made choices. We opted for the single income scenario, convinced that in the long run our family would be better off for it. We decided that having Mom home with the children was preferred over the options of placing our children in day homes or day care. That was our choice. The tradeoffs included surviving on less net disposable income than what we could have generated if we were both pursuing external careers and all the financial ramifications of that decision. We would live in a more modest home. We would drive second hand cars. The fifteen-inch black and white TV from my university days would have to do for a few more years. Accumulation of savings would be slower, if at all, in the early years. Fancy vacations? Well, they would just have to wait.

I can tell you that we never have regretted that decision. Life has unfolded beautifully and the investment in our family represented in that decision has paid us dividends over and over again with the joy and pride we experience with our children. Financially, it was tough. The early years especially when I started a new business and it took a long time for it to become established and provide us with relatively stable financial circumstances. But, there were many times when I saw my contemporaries "leave us in the dust" as they upgraded their homes, acquired their vacation homes and got the BMW and the SUV. I'll confess. I like that stuff. I like it a lot.

There were moments in our life that I would get very down on myself for not being able to keep up with what seemed like the entire world. I would get angry, resentful, envious, and jealous. Occasionally I would question the decision that we had made for Laura to stay home. I would think, "If she could just get a job and make some money it would really help." By "help" I meant "then we could get that color TV, BMW, SUV and vacation home."

There were moments when I questioned the decision. Then something would happen. I would come home from work and Laura would have my favorite supper cooked and I could smell it the moment I walked in the door. One of the children would crawl up on my lap, give me a hug and then just settle down and fall asleep right there. Someone would remind me how wonderful our family is and I would wake up and realize all of this is because of the choice we made. The choice that determined how we raised our family was more important than having two incomes. The life and pleasure we enjoy right now with our children and each other is partially built on that decision. That decision was possible because of our clarity around our priorities. When all that is clear to me, then all the regret and envy (that has long since stopped showing its ugly head) just melts away. And it was all possible because we held up our options against our priorities and then chose.

I am not suggesting that choices different than ours are wrong. That is furthest from my intent. On this very choice, today's society makes it very difficult for many people to make ends meet on just one income. We have sort of forced it upon ourselves I think. But it is real. I do not, for one second, suggest that everyone should raise a family on one income and make the hard choices necessary to make that work. Two income families are a reality. In many circumstances, they are a necessity. I know many people who have built strong marriages and raised wonderful children while balancing the challenges that come with the fiscal reality and logistical complexity of a two-income family. My respect for those who do this and do it well is immense. Good for you. There is a special place in heaven reserved for people like you.

My point is that whatever the circumstances, each couple needs to have priorities upon which to base their own decisions. Without some certainty on what is important in your shared life, my gut tells me that self preservation and self interest will fill the gap and at that point, the chance of landing on a resolution that is in the best interest of the marriage has a lower probability of being realized.

My friends did not know they did not share the same priority with respect to conflicting career opportunities until they were faced with their own challenging circumstances. When it came down to crunch time, they had nothing compelling to guide them. Their marriage was a ship without a rudder in that sense. No way to steer. So, it became every man (or woman) for himself (or herself) and the natural instincts of self preservation kicked in.

What if they had shared a common priority around careers? When faced with the opportunities, they would have had a much better chance of making a joint decision. Maybe their choice would have been that his career would always take priority because it had the higher income earning potential and that she could pursue any career opportunity that did not conflict with his career. Maybe their choice could have been that his career took priority until the children were grown, at which time she could pursue her career opportunities and he would tailor his career to allow hers to flourish. There are any number of possibilities to this if, first, the priority was that neither of them would pursue career advancement if it meant that the marriage relationship would suffer for it. The marriage would always trump financial gain.

If the marriage came first, the careers would, perhaps, but not necessarily, be less ambitious. There would not be the concern that external influences would break through that protected relationship and erode it. They would be on guard against the potential that others may question their individual commitment to their work because they were not prepared to "pay the price" or "do what it takes" for the sake of the career because when faced with that very challenge each could answer in the positive. They would say that they were not prepared to pay the price for career advancement if the price sought was the marriage. If you are not prepared to do what it takes to maintain the marriage as the priority the price will be the erosion of the marriage.

The marriage has to come first, my friend. It has to. There is no way around it. If you want to begin to experience what a truly extraordinary marriage can mean to you, the marriage comes first. Put it before yourself whenever you are facing any decision. And I do mean any decision. Then look at your choices, see how many fall away as irrelevant. See how many options do not matter. Don't rationalize your choices. Do not try to fudge the outcome. Just make a straight up call as to which of your options would be the best choice for investing in your marriage and do that one thing.

All of a sudden, it's not a sacrifice. It is what you want. It is your first choice because it supports your number one priority. Not a bad way to go through life – always getting your way.

Time to be a Couple

''When a girl marries she exchanges the
attentions of many men for the inattention of one.''

-Helen Rowland

One day you will wake up and the kids will be gone. Not gone in a sense that they are missing, just grown and on their way. It is going to happen. You know it. It is bound to. It happens to every parent eventually. Surprisingly, many of us do not prepare for it. You wake up, the kids are gone and you look to the person lying in the bed beside you and say, "Who are you?" It happens. All too much I think. I have heard this happening over and over again. I have seen it happen with close friends and family. I know that when people become so absorbed in the life of their children without protecting a portion of their own life for each other, time can zip by without ever realizing that they have forgotten each other.

Not only have they forgotten each other, they have changed independently of each other. People change. We are constantly changing. Our interests, our worries, our perceptions all change over time. Our tolerance for risk, our ambitions, our dreams and goals are all moveable and evolve with the change in our circumstances and environment. They may be bigger than before. They may be more conservative than when we were kids. It's a great dynamic this human condition we all share. Each one of us trudges along our own paths absorbing life and living. As a married couple, that path is intended to be shared. It becomes that much more dynamic because it involves the engagement of another human into our experiences. With more of us, it involves a family, extended through marriage, but more significantly, through the arrival of children. Then for the next twenty to thirty years, we have an obligation as parents to teach our children, provide them with opportunities to explore and discover their own talents, keep them alive and free of permanent scarring, both physical and emotional and then get them the heck out of the house loaded with the capacity to become self sustaining contributors to society.

During this same time we are expected to hold down a job, advance our careers, plan for retirement, get the house, get the vacation house, get the five wide screen TV's, the speed boat, the SUV, the X-box, travel the world, write the next great English novel and solve world hunger (ok, maybe not the novel or world hunger, but you get the point).

Is it any surprise to anyone that twenty-five or thirty years can fly by in a second and suddenly you wake up and realize you don't know the person lying in bed beside you? Or worse, along the way you have lost the person who should have been lying in bed beside you and she has moved on, chasing her own house, dreams, travel and novel.

How do you do all of this? How are we supposed to achieve everything that society tells us we are supposed to achieve? How do we stand proud and say to the world, "You gave me your best, world, and I did it. I got it. I've got it all" ...and still be the attentive husband that your marriage needs and your wife, rightfully, should demand.

You know what? You have to tell the world to take a hike. What the world says is important is not important. It can wait. What is important is that person who, hopefully, is still waking up beside you after twenty-five years. What is important is that after twenty-five (or forty or fifty) years you both still love waking up beside each other. What is important is that when you do wake up, you can't wait to get on with the day in this shared life that you have built together. Why? Because you have so much to do together, that you can't wait to get at it. How is that possible? It is possible because you have built that life together, one day at a time over the last twenty-five (or forty or fifty) years. You have built a relationship that is so entwined with each other that the day that is just dawning is full of promise and you cannot wait to get at it.

Well, how in the heck do you do that? Easy. Start building that life today. How do you do that? Easy. Create a life as a couple.

The marriage comes first, my friend. That is just the deal. It has to. Everything else builds from that. There is no escaping it. There is time for everything else – at least everything that matters. You can still be a great father. You can still have a very successful career. You can still get the house, the vacation home, the SUV and speed boat – if that's what you really want. You can still raise great kids and they can have a wonderful life growing up in an enriching environment and you can still achieve your retirement objectives. All of this is possible if you put your marriage first. All of this can happen and it does not have to cost you your marriage to achieve it. Your marriage is not the currency that you use to acquire all of these other trappings of a successful life. Marriage is the enabler to this success. And, an extraordinary marriage enhances all other successes and achievements by orders of magnitude because they are shared and enjoyed within a unified life as husband and wife. There is nothing better.

It is distressing to me when I see people spend their marriage for the sake of the kids. They exhaust their couple-ness chasing the next promotion. They let their relationship with their spouse atrophy while they focus on the accumulation of a retirement nest egg. What a waste. And for what? For things that are wholly achievable within a robust and energized marriage. The two are not mutually exclusive.

You have to focus your energy on your marriage. In all the busy-ness of life – the career, the friends, the kids, – you have to carve out and protect, like a religious covenant, a space that is just for you and your wife. Elsewhere in this book I talk about creating the opportunity for having time with just your wife and how you can put things in place to make that happen. Here, I am telling you that you must make it happen.

It does not have to be elaborate. It does not have to be a big production. It just has to happen, regularly, religiously, frequently. It has to be a foundation of your life. How else are you supposed to learn all that you can about this woman who is the other half of you? You are not going to learn about her dreams and wants and changes and desires and hopes and aspirations and pet peeves and quirks and hot buttons and sense of humor in the chaos of a frantic life of careers and activities and commitments. Neither one of you have time in the bulk of your waking hours to figure each other out and keep in touch with how each of you are changing when you are running around addressing all of the family requirements and schedules.

It is so important that you continue to learn about and from each other. I mentioned earlier that we all change. Well, that's the truth. I am not the same guy I was twenty-five years ago. Laura is certainly not the same woman. There are aspects of our life together now that we could not have imagined at the beginning of this journey and now, they factor significantly in our life today. Without a constant and consistent vigilance paid to the health of our couple-ness, we could very easily find ourselves at a loss to even share with each other how these things that factor so prominently into our life today effect our decisions and actions and the daily life we share.

A friend of mine once confessed to me that he was worried about a trip he was about to take with his wife. Recently retired, they had purchased a motor home and were about to embark on a two week road trip to test the new luxury on wheels. I think it was also a test for the couple to see how they would get along with each other. The anticipated road trip was going to be the longest time in thirty years that they were going to be together as a couple, with no children or friends or other family members to distract them, and he was worried about what they would talk about. "I have never spent that much time alone with just her since our honeymoon," he said, a certain degree of panic in his voice. "What do we talk about?"

"Are you kidding?" I thought. But I quickly realized he wasn't kidding. He was really concerned. They had been together for thirty years, but the life they had built together was not one of a married couple. Married, certainly, but they were married to their family and the busy inventory of commitments and activities that consumed their life. The missing ingredient was their "couple" relationship. Somewhere along the way that had been ignored and overrun by the thousand other things that consumed their time and energy.

"Talk about anything," I said. Talk about how much you love her. Tell her how beautiful she is. Tell her how wonderful she makes your life every day. Follow it up with specific examples. If you are uncomfortable with that, tell her you are uncomfortable. Declare to her that you are nervous about the whole circumstance. Chances are if you feel this way, so does she. If you do not know how to fill several hours in a vehicle driving around the country with your wife, she probably does not know what to do with you either. This sounds like a great opportunity to begin again. Accepting responsibility for not doing everything you could have or should have to nurture your relationship with her and declaring that you want to do more and understand more about what her needs and desires are is a good start. Let her know that she is the focus of your life and that after the first thirty wonderful years with her, you want to make sure that the next thirty years are even better.

Your whole road trip could be the beginning of a whole new direction in your couple life. You could examine all of the decisions that you have made along the way. This is not to say that you have made wrong decisions or bad decisions. There are many, many marriages that are good. Marriages where a husband and wife work well together as a team, raising a family, providing for themselves, focusing on solid careers, doing all the right things. They are happy. They are content.

The question to ask is not whether the marriage is good, but whether it is as good as it can be. Remember the title of this book. Your target should be the extraordinary marriage. I believe that can only happen with a truly wonderful and extraordinary relationship between two people – the husband and the wife. Everything else falls into place behind that.

So, I suggested to my friend that he focus on that. Focus on your relationship with your wife and only that. At every opportunity take the conversation to why you are in love with her. Dedicate the trip to make her happy. If you don't know what that is, don't guess. Turn it into a game. Wake up on the first day of your road trip and declare to her that today is her day. Whatever she wants, she gets. Tell her you want to do exactly what she wants to do today and every decision is hers and then support her and go with her wherever she wants to go today.

The whole experience is about learning. If you knew your wife, you could plan a day that is just for her and find things that will make her happy. If you haven't been paying attention for thirty years, you may or may not get it right. What is remarkable, when you think about it is that there are many men who have been married to their wives for a long time and probably could not plan a day just for her that is intended to touch her heart and feed her soul. Too many of us just do not take the time to learn that about our wives. We are just too busy with our own stuff or we assume that she likes the same things we do. Let me shed a little light on that for you, my friend. It is very rare that our wives like the very same things we do. Oh sure, there is bound to be an overlap. I mean, there has to be some common ground there that formed a part of the original attraction in the first place. But, my bet is that there is a lot more unshared areas of interest than you think.

I suggested to my friend that the road trip could be a great opportunity to discuss re-designing their life a little to protect more time to be a couple. It does take a commitment of effort and time to do that and if you have gone for thirty years without that discipline, it can be a habit that is difficult to make, break or create (depending on your point of view).

This example of my friend and his wife and their road trip is intended to be a surrogate for countless husbands who probably are in the same boat. Your marriage is good. Your family is functioning well. Everyone has their role to play and you have found a balance and a rhythm to your marriage and life that keeps all the balls in the air. All of that is good. Now, wouldn't you want to move that whole thing into the realm of GREAT! It can all start with you taking the first step to re-aligning your whole life and re-establishing your marriage as the priority.

I am amazed when I see couples who do not protect time for themselves. What is the point of being a couple? You do not sacrifice that relationship when you get married. You make a life time commitment to ensure that married relationship will survive for the rest of your earthly days. So, why not pay attention to it and make sure that is the case? Last time I checked, at a wedding you do not promise to merge fiscal, domestic and sexual services or support as a matter of convenience. Unless of course you had one of those "home-made" wedding vows and you actually did promise to merge for fiscal and domestic convenience, but I'll ignore that for now. If that was your intention when you promised to love and cherish each other until death do you part, then you picked the wrong game.

You promised to invest your singleness into one unified life comprised of a man and a woman. You said that you were dedicating your life to this. Well that does not happen without effort and a game plan. It does not happen through neglect or osmosis or gravity. It takes work, scheduling and commitment. If you have to, put it in your blackberry as a recurring appointment. Friday night, 7:00 pm – 12:00 pm – date with my wife. Book it and make it a priority.

Teach your children from an early age that there is space in your family's life where they are not invited. It's OK. It is actually a good thing for them to know that they are not the sole thing that is important in your life. It also makes children feel more secure and not responsible for the parents' happiness. It is important for children to witness that a relationship between husband and wife is not shared between parents and children. That is a different relationship with its own space in the family dynamic. That is OK. It is good. It is needed for the marriage.

There is nothing more important in married life than to make sure the marriage relationship is at the top of the list of priorities. You have to take care of it. You have to pay attention to it. That takes time. Think about how you spend your time on a daily, weekly, monthly, yearly basis. Do you carve out time that is protected for just you and your wife to be together? So much of what I think is important in a marriage is centered on keeping that one human relationship squarely before me when I make all my decisions. That does not mean that I exclusively consider my relationship with Laura to the exclusion of all other relevant considerations. But, it is the first thing on the list that must be considered.

For us, there is nothing more important to our relationship than time together. We have always protected that. Whether it is simply a walk in the evening or a cup of tea before bed, we find time everyday that is just for us. We are always connecting with each other. Quick phone calls during the day, a text message to each other's phones to let the other one know that we are thinking about the other person. It is an awareness of each other that is acted upon every day.

When our children were younger, finding that time and protecting it for each other was more difficult. Young children need so much of your physical time and attention. These years for a family are incredibly demanding on time and physical attention. The late teenage years and university years are exhausting for a whole other set of reasons as the children race toward adulthood and charge into the great unknown of decisions with consequences believing they are invincible. I could spend a lot of time examining that, but, it would be a distraction from the point here. The point is this. Although it may seem there are not enough hours in the day to get to everything that a young family needs from mom and dad, mom and dad still have to find a space that is reserved for each other as boyfriend and girlfriend.

Laura and I have always reserved Friday nights for ourselves. Date nights are sacred. It is a minimum requirement. I am not talking about the once a year dinner out for her birthday or your anniversary. I am talking about every Friday night. I spend a lot more time on this later in the chapter about "Tips" but for now, I implore you. If you do nothing different in your relationship with your wife resulting from your read of this book, I beg you to do this one thing – Friday night dates. Reserve it for just the two of you. No one else is invited.

I recall the days of young children in our house. Those years were exhausting. No doubt about it. Kids need a lot of attention. Help with homework, getting them to piano lessons. Making them practice their piano. There's hockey, martial arts, dance lessons, basketball, soccer, on and on and on. Then there is the refereeing that is a part of every family that has more than one child. Refereeing the constant chaos of children just being kids. Feed them. Clean them. Dress them. Read to them. Get them to sleep. Then you fall over and pass out with exhaustion.

Been there. Done that. Got the T-shirt. On top of this, you have that parent committee for the new playground. Volunteering at school, working on the Christmas pageant and once that's done, you go straight into preparation for the spring concert.

Don't forget the careers now. You've got to fit in the work you brought home. Or, for many parents, it's off to the second job in the evening or weekend to help cover the extra bills for the unexpected washer and dryer that was required when the old set finally gave up the ghost. And thank God for the new washer and dryer, because the mountain of laundry isn't taking care of itself. In between the wash and rinse cycle you can wash the kitchen floors, do the dishes, clean the toilets, repair the lawn mower, cut the grass, change the oil in the van. Shall I keep going? The list is never ending. It is relentless. There's barely room for a special project like replacing the shingles on the garage roof.

Hey, life is busy. Who's got time to be a couple? The answer is – you do. You have to. In the midst of all this, hopefully, joyous chaos of family, you must find time to be a couple.

I was driving in a vehicle with three colleagues one week before Valentine's Day. I asked the others, "What are you doing for Valentine's Day?" After the laughter subsided I said, "No, seriously, what are you doing for your wife on Valentine's Day?" The first husband said, "Nothing." The second's reaction was to just laugh again. The third husband said that he and his son were going skiing. "But, my wife and daughter went to a spa last week, so they are OK," he added. BONK! Wrong! Whoever said Valentine's Day is a Hallmark Holiday and not legitimate is just trying to find general support for a failure to take an obvious opportunity to make your wife feel special.

One of the best ways to create and sustain that feeling of intimacy as a couple is to constantly create opportunities to make your wife feel special as a woman. And it is so easy to do. It doesn't have to be big. It can be very small. But, I will give you a really good idea that you can take to the bank. Do not work on your wife's birthday, Valentine's Day or your anniversary. If your wife works outside the home (or for that matter even if she is a stay at home mom) convince her that she has to take those days off too. Reserve those days for yourselves only. Arrange for someone to take care of your children and just disappear for the day, doing whatever the two of you may love to do. Alternatively, you can plan an entire day just for your wife to cater to her special interests. Spoil her completely. I have done this for Laura and it is great. I talk about this more later in this book. You can do this, too. It's up to you. I highly recommend that you consider protecting these days for you as a couple. At least it creates, at a minimum, some time for just the two of you.

I never work on these three days of the year. These days are reserved for Laura and me only. No one else is invited, especially on the anniversary and Valentine's Day. Often on the birthday the kids are involved at some point, but these days are free of work and they are focused on our relationship as a couple.

Never stop courting your wife, my friend. She was first your girlfriend. You did all kinds of goofy things just to get her attention. You worked at keeping her interested in you. In one way or another, you wooed her. You pursued her. Then, you managed to get her to agree to marry you. What then? Do you just stop? So many times it seems we think that the job ends with getting married. The truth is, it is just beginning. You have only planted the seed. Now you have to tend it, nurture it, make it grow before it can bear real fruit.

I have never stopped courting my bride. I try to make her fall in love with me again and again all the time. I never want to stop making her feel special. I want her to always know that she is my one true love and that I will do anything for her. I want her to feel that she is being pursued, wooed. I want her to feel that she is desired as a woman. I want her to be excited about Friday night. I want the feeling of anticipation and potential for romance.

I do not buy into the idea that all of that youthful heart fluttering must end. Of course we are not walking around like star struck teenagers, incapacitated with infatuation, but it is thrilling when waves of infatuation still come over me. It still happens. At fifty years old, I can still feel that fluttering heart of excitement with my bride. I don't want it to die. And I especially don't want it to die for Laura. I want her to feel loved for herself as a woman. Not as a mother, a friend, partner, domestic manager or anything else that involves others. I want her to know that there is a place in our life where it is still about us, our life long courtship, our relationship as one man and one woman.

The time together has to be physically together, too. Talking on the phone and emails do not count unless you are geographically separated because one of you is on the road with your work. I understand that. That really is part of our reality since I spend many days on the road with my work. In those circumstances, phones and emails are all we have to connect.

Laura and I have always found time for each other. Over time, Friday night dates expanded to the occasional over-night date or twenty-four hour date away from the responsibilities of children and family. We exchanged twenty-four hours of babysitting with other young parents in our same circumstances to create these windows of opportunity. I encourage you to find a balanced relationship with friends and family to create these opportunities for each other. Over time, as our children became young adults with the independence that came with that, we were able to expand the twenty-four hour date into weekends and holidays where Laura and I could get away and enjoy each other.

The weekend get-a-ways and holidays we enjoy at this stage of our life would not be possible without focusing on Friday nights and other short term opportunities to be together early in our marriage. The investment in creating and protecting those couple moments early in our marriage helped us build a marriage relationship that is evidenced by a couple who like being together and have endless things they want to do together. We have limitless conversations. We want to be together. It's fun. Time together is easy. It's great.

If you are ever thinking that a road trip with just your wife is a daunting proposition because you are not sure what you would talk about, then you should do something about that now so that when the road trip comes up, you are looking forward to it. Start small. Start with thirty minutes over a cup of coffee at your friendly neighborhood coffee shop. Stretch it to lunch. Take your time. Pretend you are dating again. In fact, that is what you are doing. If you have not nurtured this one-on-one relationship with your bride, then it may not exist right now. You have to start building it from scratch. Now, you do have an advantage in that it is not like you do not know each other. There is no need to walk up to her and try to get her phone number like you were trying to pick up some hottie in a bar. (Although, the role playing is not a bad idea for something fun to do one night!)

When the last child moves out on his or her own, I want each married couple to look at each other and scream," YEAH BABY! Let's play!" rather than ask "Who are you?" There is only one way to make that happen. Create time for just each other every day. Be a couple first. All your other hats that you must wear – daddy, provider, career guy, plumber, electrician, gardener, auto mechanic, home repair expert, disciplinarian, teacher – all the roles you play during the course of your life will fit much better into your life if you are first a husband, attentive lover and best friend to that woman you promised to share one life with. Together, as a true couple, all the other responsibilities of life fall into place and, I believe, you can be better in your other roles if you take care of this most important role first.

OK. Maybe loving your wife will not make you a better auto mechanic, but, really, who cares about that, unless you actually are an auto mechanic.

Nothing Says "I Love You" Like Separate Vacations!

> "Do you know what it means to come home at night to a woman who'll give you a little love, a little affection, a little tenderness? It means you're in the wrong house, that's what it means."
>
> -Henny Youngman

Right after a chapter dedicated to being a couple, you probably think I am flip-flopping when the very next chapter title promotes separate vacations. Well there is method in my madness. Trust me. It all makes sense when you look at it as a complete package.

Friends of ours have been married about twenty years. They have no children. It's just the two of them and they have a wonderful relationship as far as I can tell. Because it is just the two of them, one could imagine that they could get on each others' nerves from time to time without the need to deal with children and family demands on a regular basis. There is no Mommy's taxi service or volunteering at the school. There are no demands for coaching T-ball or helping kids with homework. At least with children running around the house, if you are not paying attention, you don't get on each other's nerves because you are too busy to notice the other person's nerves, let alone "get on them". That's a whole other issue which is what I talked about in the previous chapter. Part of being a couple is, in fact, getting on each other's nerves. That is going to happen sometimes no matter what you do. Like it or not, you will not always like each other. Sometimes your wife will just lean on your one good nerve and sometimes you will do it to her.

A great couple will learn how to minimize that experience and will also learn how to fix it when it occurs. You will respect each other's nerves and learn how to get off them once you are on them.

But, for now, let's focus on this idea of respecting each other's space as well. Back to my friends. Let's call them Sam and Rita. (Not their real names – it's a witness protection requirement!). For Sam, it is just Rita every day, all day. And Rita only has Sam. That can be a very difficult dynamic for a couple at times. There is nothing to distract you away from the minute quirks of the other that can magnify in your mind and just drive you crazy.

When there's just the two of you, it is pretty easy to just lean on the one good nerve remaining like a dentist's drill on an impacted molar without any laughing gas! Hey, we are only human after all. We all get on each others' nerves and we all need our own space from time to time. Rita often describes the balance they have found with each other as giving each other space in their togetherness. I don't know if she came up with that phrase or adopted it as her own. The source of the turn of phrase is not important to me. What is important is the truth of it. Correctly applied to a relationship, it is a very powerful way to enhance the strength of a marriage.

Warped into something unintended and taken to extremes, it can literally kill a marriage.

Laura and I are married. We are not joined at the hip! We did not give up being individuals when we got married. We chose to bring our lives together to create something greater and I think we are achieving that. Of course our work is not done. It is never going to be done. Until death do us part. That is the deal for us both.

However, we also do not defend our respective individualism at the cost of advancing the marriage. It is not a win-lose kind of thing. My individualism is not diminished because I am married. It is stronger because I am committed to my marriage. I am committed to something that is so important it actually helps define my individualism and frames my life.

I am sure you have heard this before. "Marriage isn't going to change me. I'm still going to do what I want to do, when I want to do it." Maybe you have even said this. If you are one of those guys who have said this, then, I have to be honest with you. Only if you have said this as a joke, with your wife present would I accept this or anything remotely close to this as a legitimate contribution to a conversation. If, however, you are a guy who actually believes this, either as a mantra for your life or even in the smallest of ways applicable to your life after your wedding day, then, frankly, you are dreaming! (I actually wanted to say "you are an idiot", but my wife said it was too harsh).

I cannot be any clearer than that. You are dreaming (and by that I mean you are an idiot) if you think that marriage is not going to change you. It will definitely change you. It will either change you into a husband who is treasured or an ex-husband who is trashed. I am picking just the two extremes of the continuum, but there are many degrees and options in between, like the ambivalent husband going through the motions or the man married to the woman who only feels indifference toward him. If your marriage does not change you, then you are missing the greatest opportunity of your life to discover something that can be so fulfilling and enriching that your entire outlook on the world is altered for the better.

So, how do we nurture our individualism while investing completely in this marriage relationship? Are the two not inconsistent? Don't you sacrifice your individualism when you get married? That's the deal right?

Not at all. Stand up comedians love to abuse the marriage relationship with their jokes. And, to be sure, there is a lot to laugh about in marriage. The laughter should be an ocean in which we swim throughout our married life. Many of the jokes are of the beleaguered husband or the Mars/Venus differences of men and women which are presented as inexplicably conflicting and confusing.

I do not underestimate the challenge of understanding another human being as intimately as is required for a husband and wife to grow together. That's the great thing about the whole relationship. It takes a lifetime to sort out. No, correct that: it takes a lifetime of growing together. We never actually ever sort it all out.

It seems to me that a truly successful marriage includes a combination of individual and shared interests and pursuits. It has to. It is not natural for any two people to do all the same things together all the time. It is not natural that two people will like all the same things in exactly the same way with the exact same intensity. It is not natural that two people will want to spend every moment of their entire life together. None of that is natural or, in my view, healthy.

Everyone needs their own space. A great marriage respects and accommodates that. Each person in the marriage uses his or her own space for his or her own purposes to fulfill their need to be an individual. Individualism is not a withdrawal from the marriage relationship. In fact, it is the opposite. Positive individualism contributes to the strength of the marriage. The two nourish each other.

Laura and I have many, many interests that we share. We have nurtured these interests and developed them over the years. I know when we are in our retirement years we will not be bored. We will not look at each other and wonder "What is she/he doing here?" We have many things we like to do together – paint, music, travel, work with charities and many more. We also have individual interests that we each support, but do not participate in. I am into endurance racing. I enjoy running marathons, ultra-marathons and triathlons. Laura does not. I enjoy my work on the boards of directors of a couple of charities. Laura does not. We both have a private trainer, but we work out separately. Laura is focused on developing her original music and performing. I am not. Laura enjoys her book club, scrapbooking and photography. I enjoy the products of Laura's efforts, but have no interest in the actual activity required to produce photo albums and scrapbooks. Laura likes to go on retreats. I do not. She enjoys going to some concerts that I have no desire to see and I enjoy the occasional round of golf with friends. We both have our separate annual trips that we take without the other.

I have been attending a golf weekend with seven buddies every April for the last seventeen years. I have only missed one annual trip because of work commitments – year sixteen. But every year, for the last weekend in April my friends and I travel to Kelowna, British Columbia for four days of golf. It is a great and exhausting weekend and I love it. My good friend had asked me for years prior to ever going on the golf weekend to join him. I always declined, citing economics as the reason. "We just can't afford it," I would say. But, I have to admit now that it was not just the money. I just felt guilty about taking the time for myself and leaving Laura at home alone with the children. Laura eventually convinced me that it was alright to have this time just for myself and to go on the golf weekend. So, I went. Now it is a part of the routine of our life and I enjoy it completely.

Every year since our girls were born Laura has travelled alone to Windsor, Ontario for about twelve days at the end of May. Her "annual sabbatical", as it has become known, is used to visit family and friends. Laura stays with her parents and reconnects with her family and childhood friends.

Laura's annual sabbatical originally came up to address Laura's homesickness. When our daughters were born, Laura was feeling particularly homesick and so I purchased a plane ticket for her to visit her home town and I held the fort down at home with the four kids. She resisted going for the same reason I resisted the golf weekend. She didn't want to leave me "burdened" with the kids all alone.

In each case, we both resisted taking some time for just our-selves. In each situation, the principal reason was the same, concern for the other person left behind. Ultimately, the one who was staying behind convinced the other that it was OK to enjoy that time away from the responsibilities of the mar-riage and family and to enjoy herself or himself and that time with friends without regret or guilt. Just simply enjoy the time away.

This is one of the greatest gifts I think we have ever given each other. Our favorite gift for each other is time together and our second best gift for each other is time apart. I cannot imagine our life without these two windows. They are as solid in our annual calendars as are our birthdays or anniversary. Now, after so many years, we both enjoy our individual trips without any guilt or concern. We are completely comfortable with creating space and time for our individualism and respecting each others' space.

A few weeks ago Laura and I were at a social function and just talking to friends when one woman mentioned that she was going away for a weekend with a few girlfriends to celebrate their shared milestone birthday. They all turn thirty this year! She mentioned that last year they all went away for a weekend, leaving their husbands at home with the children while the girls spent a weekend doing what women do. Nothing exotic. They just were together away from the responsibilities of wife and mother for two days. It was the first time any of them had done such a thing and they loved it so much, they decided to do it again this year.

It sounded like a good idea to me and a lot of fun for both the women and the husbands. It gave the husbands a golden opportunity to create a special experience for themselves and their children that could only be accomplished without Mom in attendance.

I expect this would be equally true for Mom and the kids when Dad is away. In homes where both parents are holding down careers outside the home, creating these opportunities for both parents is a very good idea. It revitalizes the individual who can get away from the sometimes overwhelming requirements of a family and allows the other parent the chance to play with the kids within a completely different and rare dynamic.

Our home is more traditional in the sense that my career has been, for all intents and purposes, the sole source of family income and Laura has been a stay at home mother. There have been stages in our marriage when Laura was working outside the home, but, for the most part, since the arrival of children, Laura has mostly been at home with the kids. So, my being away for a weekend to golf with my buddies has not created the same opportunity for Laura to cultivate a relationship with the children since she has been there every day for them in the normal flow of life. In my case though, a week or more with just the children while Mom was away presented all sorts of possibilities. The stories that flow from those experiences will have to wait for another time.

The point here is that both Laura and I have discovered that our individualism survives the wedding vows and in our case, it has flourished. We both respect the other person's individualism and the right to feed that individualism so that it never disappears.

For me, having separate interests is absolutely critical to a healthy marriage. It is as important as having an absolute commitment to share one life together as a married couple. The two are not inconsistent with each other. They co-exist beautifully if you allow them to. One compliments the other and each allows the other to flourish. Neither is starved for lack of attention.

The magic is in the balance between. We invest our respective single lives to acquire a shared life on our wedding day. We spend the rest of our life nurturing that shared life. Part of nurturing that one shared life is creating spaces in your togetherness to let each other's individuality grow and strengthen. Seems like a tricky balance, doesn't it? Only tricky, I believe, if you confuse singleness with individuality.

They are not the same. Not even close. Singleness is being unattached to another person. Individuality is who you are and exists both as a single person and a full participant and partner in a marriage. Singleness is gone once you are married. You spend your singleness to acquire a marriage. Singleness cannot exist inside a successful marriage. It is counterproductive to a truly committed marriage. However, individualism cannot only thrive inside a marriage, it is required. A truly great marriage needs each person to have a strong personal identity. There is no better place to discover and grow your own individualism than within a fully supportive and loving marriage. It is all a matter of balance.

The balance comes from the shared mutual respect and agreed upon priorities of the marriage. For instance, I would never go on my golf weekend if for some reason Laura really needed me. And she would never think of going on her annual sabbatical if I needed her. The marriage would always win out as the priority. But, we also both know that neither of us would ask the other one to give up his or her annual get-a-way for something trivial or unnecessary. We both know this and the trust shared in our relationship allows us to make the shared decision to pursue individual interests within the marriage and not in spite of the marriage.

My marriage is going to change me. It has changed me. I am counting on it continuing to do so. That's the only way I can become a better person on this earth. Just as I say I do not sacrifice for my marriage I can also say my individuality is stronger because I spent my singleness to acquire a share in this one married life.

I Always Win!
Or...
A Good Argument is A Great Way
to Love!

"Marriage is an adventure, like going to war."

-G. K. Chesterton

Husbands and wives disagree. We argue. We tick each other off. We cannot get away from it. It happens. Anger happens. Disappointment and frustration and "I just don't like you right now" all happen. So do feelings of "Get out of my face", "Do it yourself", "Leave me out of it" and "Leave me alone".

One of the harshest lines I have ever heard about marriage is a line delivered by Steve Martin in the movie "Parenthood". Steve's character has just been passed over for the promotion to partner in his advertising firm after working like crazy on a big new account at the expense of spending time with his children and wife. This was his big chance to reach that next rung on the corporate ladder. It was snapped away from him and given to the new, hot, ambitious single guy. He felt used and manipulated and not valued by the partners of his firm. In his frustration and anger, Steve's character quits his job in the heat of the moment and heads home. Upon arriving home he is hit with all sorts of normal family issues. We have all seen them, either in our own lives as parents or as children. They represent the normal chaos of raising a family. If Steve would have received his promotion, he could have handled all of it with love and joy. He would have been walking on air. But, that was not where he was. He was at the lowest of low emotionally. His confidence and self image as a man, husband, father and provider were at an all time low.

He arrives home, rants about the entire experience to his wife, played by Mary Steenbergen. He was looking for her support, but she had other things on her mind. When she questioned the wisdom of his decision to quit his job at this point in their tenuous financial circumstance he pushed back, angry at her for not supporting him.

"But," she said. "I'm pregnant." – an unexpected pregnancy that only magnifies the financial stress his rash decision had imposed on the family. He was so wound up with the anger and frustration of the career implosion that he could not even approach the idea about being happy about the surprise pregnancy. The argument got worse with both husband and wife taking shots at each other completely in reaction to the tension that existed from the circumstances. They were both clearly outside of the ordinary rhythm of their life, because somehow, as the audience watched this scene unfold, we got the feeling that these two people were, notwithstanding the immediate circumstances, happy together. They were just not happy at that moment. Steve then said that he had to go and take one of their children to little league.

"Do you have to?" asked Mary, feeling a need to work through the conflict and unfortunate situation they had suddenly discovered for themselves. And then Steve responded with one of the most cutting lines I have ever heard about the accumulated pressures and challenges of balancing and succeeding at all times simultaneously as a successful career person, father and husband.

Mary asked, "Do you have to go?" and, as he left the room to take his son to his little league game, he turned around and hissed through his teeth, "My whole life is 'have to'".

Ouch! I am sure that many of us have had many moments in our lives when things were just not going exactly as we would have liked and we can identify with Steve's character at that moment. Sometimes it feels that way. Sometimes we are just angry at the world and sometimes that leads to arguments with our wives. At times I have felt like I am completely dissatisfied with my entire life. The feeling is not real. It is just a frustration that pushes a bunch of junk emotion forward and I roll around in it for a while. Not long though because I know it is not real. It is a bunch of nonsense that fortunately does not take root with me. But, every once in awhile, a little self pity finds its way into my heart.

I know the frustration Steve's character was feeling. I have never quit a job in anger and frustration, but I have been fired from my job – more than once. It's not a good feeling. It cuts to the core of your feeling of personal worth, especially when you are the sole bread winner for the family. It is a very scary feeling. It is a challenge to keep your cool and still be the good person you are when you feel like a piece of crap.

It does not take a job loss for a person to be very vulnerable and not at their best. We all have days where we are just not right with ourselves for any number of reasons. It does not take much. Sometimes, any little thing can just set us off and before you know it, you are angry at anything and everything in your path. In a marriage, most often the first thing in your path is your wife. So, what do you do? You attack! You take it out on her. You are just mad and she is the closest target. Before you know it, your wife is mad, too. Now you are both mad. Who cares why you are mad. You just are.

The dishes are not done.

Whose shoes are these piled up at the door and why do I have to keep tripping over them?

Can someone just once turn the laundry over without being asked?

Who put my favorite blouse in the dryer? Now it will only fit a four year old with abnormally long arms.

I don't want leftovers again.

The car is acting up again.

The washer is broken.

The toilet is running.

The in-laws are coming to stay with us for a month in the summer.

The bank called. We are overdrawn again.

I didn'tlikethewayyoujokedaboutusatthedinnerpartytonight.

Why didn't you know that I was upset?

Do you have to go out of town again?

It's your turn to deal with the kids. I'm too tired.

You don't pay enough attention to me?

Do you have any idea how much stress I am under at work?

You think this is easy?

Why don't you try doing my job for just one day?

We haven't made love in two weeks!

Would somebody other than me take out the garbage just once!

I'm too fat.

No you are not too fat.

What do you mean by that?

What do I mean by what?

You think I'm fat.

I never said you were fat.

Yes you did.

No I didn't.

Yes you did.

You said I was not TOO fat. So, you think I am fat.

I never said that. I said you were not fat.

No you didn't. You said I wasn't too fat. That means you think I am fat, just not too fat. You think I am fat, just not obese.

I never said that.

Well, do you think I am fat?

No I do not think you are fat. I mean, you are not skinny, but you are not fat.

So, I am not skinny. Just "plump"! Is that what you think? You think I am plump. So, I am on the way to being fat.

I never said that.

Yes you did.

Who cares?

You don't care about me?

You are beautiful.

You mean for a fat person.

No I don't. I mean for you. For me. You are perfect for me.

That's a cop out.

(Silence)

Fine. I'm fat. I just won't eat anymore.

Won't eat? That's ridiculous.

Oh so now I am "ridiculous". I'm just some ridiculous, fat slob that you are stuck with.

....Need I go on!

Any one of these things, however minor they may be, can cause an argument to erupt instantaneously. I am not even talking about the big things that come along. I mean the really big things that can shake a marriage to its core. All of this stuff is just the normal stuff of everyday life. But, it can still throw you. Depending how you handle the little stuff, you will either equip yourself to succeed in handling the big stuff or you will find yourself in a situation where you cannot overcome the big challenges that are certain to throw themselves into your path at some point in your life.

By the way, the small stuff is not small at all. Refusing to put the toothpaste cap back on the tube when you know it drives your wife crazy demonstrates a lack of respect. How hard can it be to just change that irritating little behavior and invest in building mutual respect? Laura is very big on recycling. Where there is one garbage pail in our house, there are two – one for "real garbage" and one for recyclables. I am not as diligent about sorting the garbage as Laura would like. It is not that I don't care about the environment. I just don't pay as close attention to it as she does. I am getting better at it. Not because I want to. Because it matters to Laura. Laura does the same thing for me, too. She knows what I like and don't like and she always seems to accommodate my quirks effortlessly.

It's the little hiccups and conflicts in our life that provide us a great opportunity to show our wives how much we love them. If we do this well, when the big ugly things come along, we will be well rehearsed and well equipped to handle those issues with love and compassion and unity.

What happens when a conflict arises? One person challenges the other in some way. Right away our natural tendency is to go to the defensive. We put up our guard. We hunker down and get ready to defend. We counter with a jab here or there. We may take the tact that the best defense is a strong offense and attack with our own ... "Oh yeah! Well you... blahblahblah." Let me tell you something. None of that works. None of that gets to a mutually satisfying resolution of the conflict. It will not help you understand the conflict, the core or root of the disagreement and it will not facilitate finding a shared and agreed resolution of the issue. It will not address your separate and common emotional needs.

Before contemplating this chapter I never really thought through the process of conflict resolution that Laura and I use to address our disagreements. It is just something that we both do together and we always seem to get to a finish line that is satisfactory to both of us.

Now, conflict resolution is something I know something about. In my corporate life a big part of what I do to earn my daily bread is conflict resolution. The most important thing about conflict resolution is to know your audience. You must understand what is important to the participants in the conflict and how they receive and process information. The more you understand how people think and perceive their world, the better your chance of finding a place of resolution for a disagreement. At the very least, you will be able to identify very clearly what the core of the conflict is and be able to precisely define what the difference is between those involved with the conflict so that at the end of it all you can at least agree as to what you are disagreeing about. Sometimes that is a good place to land. Inevitably, the disagreement is much narrower in scope and far less extreme than what may be originally contemplated when the argument began.

The art and science of communication is critical to dealing with conflict. It should be of no surprise to anyone that although it is more dramatic and it may feel really good right at the moment, yelling, screaming, throwing things or storming out of the room rarely is successful in advancing to a point of resolution unless the storming out is the safest way to deal with pent up anger and staying in the room may lead to some sort of physical, emotional or other personal hurt being inflicted on the other person. In that case, by all means, storm out until you are calm enough to deal with the issue at hand without any such threat. But, you have to return and deal with the situation constructively and timely. Give yourself five to twenty minutes – tops – then get back in there and deal with it.

For me, with any argument or disagreement with Laura, winning isn't everything. It's the only thing. How's that for a "stick your neck out" statement? Don't worry. I haven't lost my mind. Not yet. Well, not to the point where I am a threat to society anyway. But I mean what I said. I like to win. The important thing to understand with this is my definition of "winning".

There is no win in an argument if at the end of it either one of us is dissatisfied with the outcome. There is no win if either one of us is hurt. There is no win if we just bury the disagreement without resolution. There is no win if at the end of the dispute we are not holding each other lovingly and meaning it. So, winning an argument is everything to me. Being right about a dispute is not. (Although I still like being right.) I would rather be resolved and sleeping together in our bedroom than right and sleeping alone on the couch. If you insist on maintaining that you are right, I think you are destined to spend a lot of time alone.

Getting to a satisfactory resolution is the most important thing about a disagreement with my wife. For the outcome to be satisfying, we both have to accept it without reservation or regret. The resolution is absolute and complete. There is no keeping score for future disputes. There is no, "I'll give you this one, but you owe me." None of that nonsense. There is no score sheet in our marriage. That would imply that there is a "me against you" somewhere in our relationship and that is just impossible because together we are living one life. Any me versus you dynamic suggests that we have not bought into the whole reality of investment of our individual singleness's into one unified life. That just doesn't work. Any healthy marriage respects individualism. The mechanics and rhythm of a marriage can respect and demonstrate that in any number of ways. But, at the core of the marriage there should not be any me against you type of thinking – unless you are talking about a game of Scrabble. In that case, there are no holds barred. If you are playing Scrabble in our house, you are going down, baby!

I mentioned earlier that understanding your audience is critical in dealing with conflict. A lot of investment in professional training goes into grooming people for managing conflict in the corporate world. People make their livings teaching and training about conflict resolution. It's big business. A lot of people do the same with married couples. Counseling and mediation is often designed to help couples learn how to address conflict, providing them with the tools they need to help themselves work together, live together, love together and hopefully build a stronger marriage together. Anyone really struggling with the challenges of conflict resolution in their marriage should certainly take advantage of any professional support they can access to help them learn how to deal with conflict. There are lots of very good methods and tools available to you that can really help with this challenge. The marriage is worth the investment.

In your marriage, it is really important to understand how your wife works, how she thinks, how she receives information and processes that information. You have got to understand your woman. As ridiculous as that sounds given the long and well established history that men never seem to understand women, you have got to put the effort into getting to know her very, very well.

We have all been in that mystical place of utter confusion and befuddlement when it comes to trying to understand the complexities of another person – especially our wives. It is a constant mystery. Some mystery is great, even preferred. I love it when Laura surprises me with something new about herself. It is great to know that after thirty years of dating and marriage, she can still surprise me. That's just fun. But the whole experience does not have to be a complicated mystery that is impossible to unravel and understand. That is just frustrating. It is possible to learn how to communicate better with your wife if you take time to understand and learn what is most effective for her.

There are many psychological tests and tools that can be used that identify how a person's mind works. One of the most recognized models is the Myers Briggs personality test. This test has been around for a long time and by answering a relatively few basic questions about choice in a number of proposed circumstances, your natural tendencies are identified. You can go on the internet and take a quick test right now and it will tell you what your natural tendencies are.

For instance, the test may ask you if you would rather spend your Saturday night at a cocktail party with thirty people or have a quiet dinner party with a few close friends. Other possible questions would be if you like to follow established rules or whether it is easy to get excited about something or if you like a lot of details before you make a decision. Your answers to these and a myriad of other questions will help determine if you are more naturally an introvert or an extrovert. Are you a sensing person or an intuitive person? Are you a person who judges or perceives? Do you wait for additional information? Do you make your decisions based upon information (thinking) or emotions (feeling)? Once you have done that, then there is information that tells you how a person who is a introvert, sensing, perceptive thinking (an "ISPT") person processes information and functions. It will also show how this type of person thinks and functions differently than an extrovert, intuitive, judging, feeling ("ENJF") person. Understanding you and your wife's Myers Briggs profile can help you both understand how the other person works and can help explain why you sometimes disconnect with each other. It may also help resolve some circumstances that have previously led to conflict.

Another test is based on colors. Have you ever had your colors done? (And I don't mean whether you look better in fall or spring colors.) This tool uses a series of questions to categorize you into four basic personality types – thoughtful, emotional, analytical and judgmental. It works on similar principals to the Myers-Briggs tool and helps people understand people. There are several very useful personality tools that can help you not only understand yourself, but also understand other people. These tools also help you learn to identify individual natural tendencies and how people receive information. By information, I mean all types of social inputs including spoken language, body language, moods, everything that contributes to a person's understanding or perception of a particular situation or social dynamic. Basically, it is how we think and feel and process information and respond and form opinion and influence emotions and make choices. It is how we work as human beings.

The good news about all of these different tools is that there is no right or wrong answer to any of the questions or any of the outcomes. They just simply assist you in understanding how you think and function and they can be very helpful in understanding how other people think and function. For instance, I am a "big picture" kind of person. I am willing to make decisions and act on those decisions with very little information. I think that makes me an "orange" in the color system. As I get more information, my perception of the situation can change and I can make another very different decision and act on it. That can really rub a "blue" person (someone who likes a lot of detail and analysis before they make their decision) the wrong way. And, they can view my willingness to change my opinion and actions based on new information as completely frustrating because they like to sort it all out, make one decision, pick one path and carry it out without amendment to the plan. They have to sort out the path from A to B before they take step one and then march straight to B from A without deviation. Me? I don't care how we get to B just as long as we get there.

I often tell my co-workers to not give me a little information and ask for my views, because I will come to a conclusion based on whatever information I've got and move on it. Sometimes, because of this natural tendency, I move too fast. Being aware of that in myself, I have learned to manage that tendency and have built a discipline of double checking information and asking for more thorough information. It doesn't always work. But, being aware of my natural tendency is important to managing the circumstances around me.

Being aware of my natural tendencies and those of my wife is very helpful on the home front. Laura is an analytical person. She likes to dig into the details of a situation, understand and analyze the nuances before she is ready to talk about a decision or resolution. I just jump ahead to the finish line, come to a conclusion and I am good to go.

If I were to insist on treating every dispute in a manner that best suits my natural tendencies, Laura would always be dissatisfied with the outcome because she would not have the opportunity to think through the details of it and analyze it. That would be a loss to me because even though I would have been done with it for myself, Laura would still be struggling alone with the issue. It may eventually get resolved for her as well, but there is a very good chance that, acting independently of each other, we may each resolve the issue differently. Ultimately, we would not be unified in the outcome of the dispute and that would be a chink in the armor of our marriage. However minor it may seem, that chink would, along with other chinks accumulated over time, weaken the relationship. That's not good.

I do not want to paint a picture that suggests it is impossible for any single human to figure this all out and understand it. I don't have to. It is just true. None of us will ever figure it all out. That's half the fun of the whole journey! However, being aware of our own personal natural tendencies as well as those of others can be very helpful in dealing with all kinds of situations. I have been fortunate in that as a benefit to my years working my way up the corporate ladder, I was exposed to many opportunities to learn about this stuff and apply it to my own professional and personal life. Not everyone gets this opportunity. Many people don't even know that these differences exist. I suggest that if you are struggling in your communication with your wife, start by talking to her directly. You may just need to learn more about how each of you is wired. That may help clear up a lot of misunderstanding and frustration.

In the corporate world, at some point in your career, depending on your chosen career path, often knowing what you know as a technical expert (accountant, lawyer, engineer, scientist) becomes less and less relevant than how well you understand people and interact with people. Eventually, in my experience, success in the corporate environment (assuming you define success as rising to the top or near top of the corporate food chain – the hallowed corner executive office) most often requires a deft ability to work with people. The more you understand people, the more likely you will succeed in your relationships with them.

Is it any surprise that understanding your wife and working with her is a natural pre-requisite to rising to the top of the marriage food chain – the extraordinary marriage? Why would we spend so much time investing in improving our people skills in the office and not dedicate at least the same effort, if not more, for our relationships at home? It is one of the best investments we can make. It is just part of a standard maintenance program for your single most important investment – *your life*. You have invested your life into this marriage. Why would you not want to maintain it? If you don't, it is like buying that rare vintage automobile and then letting it sit out in the weather without protecting it or maintaining it. Eventually your investment will rust out and not run. What a waste! Same deal for your marriage. You have to take care of it. It is a precious thing. Invest in a good maintenance program and watch its value grow immeasurably over time. The payoffs will never stop flowing to you.

There are lots of ways to learn more about how you and your wife work. Many books and programs help people recognize the differences between men and women and can help you understand the differences and similarities between you and your wife specifically. I encourage you to seek these resources out and use them. If all else fails, just sit down and talk to your wife. When you are both in a good place, just sit down and talk about how each of you reacts to conflict without having to try and deal with a conflict. Just talk about what happens inside you, your thought processes, your emotions, what helps you understand conflict, what helps her resolve the issue within herself. Just taking time to try and understand may lead to very different behaviors and results when you do have a conflict.

Or.... you can just do the Cosmo quiz every month for about a year with each other.

Understanding each other's natural tendencies and how they work together (or clash) can help you manage conflict so much better. Just pounding the table and insisting that the other person see and perceive the world just like you is the recipe for disaster. If you keep doing that, the results will be the same. Doing it harder and faster and louder does not make it any better if your wife just is not wired to receive what you are trying to communicate. You know the old expression – the definition of insanity is doing the same thing over and over again and expecting different results. Think about it!

With Laura and me, I realize that there are a few sacred "Rules of Engagement" that factor into our disputes. These rules have always been unspoken between us. Thinking about it, though, I realize that they are there. We have just never had the need to codify them before. They are just true and they help us engage in healthy arguments.

In our arguments we can actively love each other. That is really important. How do we do this? Well, it involves a number of truths – assumptions and behaviors – that exist between Laura and me. These truths create a safe place for us to work out our disagreements with confidence.

1.   We never push the other person's hot buttons. I say "never", but I know neither one of us has a perfect track record on that. But, I have to admit, I think our track record is pretty good on it. You know your respective wife's hot buttons. It is also so tempting, especially if you get a sense that you may be losing the battle, to go for a hot button – a hit below the belt to try and regain some lost ground. Well, just don't do it. This is never going to help the situation immediately and will sustain an injury into the future that will certainly impact your wife's confidence in your relationship and feelings of security. It's a cheap shot. Nothing is gained by doing it and it erodes your marriage.

2.   We both know that whatever the conflict is, that neither one of us would ever consciously do anything to hurt the other person. That's just not a possibility. That's not to say that we do not unconsciously hurt the other person, but never intentionally. If I become aware that anything I do or say causes Laura any hurt, I am immediately regretful and the behavior is stopped. Period. The intent is that it is stopped forever (but for my imperfect relapses over time). The same is true the other way. Then, if the situation

ever arises where I am perceiving hurt from Laura, I can stop and say, "Wait a minute. Laura would never do anything to consciously hurt me so, either I do not understand what I am perceiving or Laura is not aware that what she is doing is hurting me." That gives us a starting point to first of all understand the situation better and get on the path of resolution.

3.   There is never any threat of physical hurt of any kind. No excuses. No exceptions.

4.   No insults or personal attacks of any kind. Emotional and intellectual hurt is just as real as physical hurt. That just cannot happen.

5.   In all circumstances we rely upon our shared and agreed priorities. What does our faith say about this? What is best for us as a couple? What is best for our family? Sometimes that may mean the outcome feeds the needs of one of us more than the other, but that, too, is an investment in the couple and we know that sometimes feeding one of us is needed at that particular time.

6.   I do not have to be right.

7.   Neither do you.

8.   If I am honest about expressing how I feel, I cannot be wrong. How I feel is how I feel. You do not have to agree with it, but I cannot be wrong. It is my feeling. I may be wrong on the facts or my perception may be off because of a lack of understanding of the facts, but my feelings are mine.

9. We are determined to get to a resolution that respects both of us. We both want to find a way to make the other person feel OK again.

10. We will apologize sincerely when appropriate.

11. We will always accept an apology without reservation or conditions.

12. We talk about what we have learned and how that will help to minimize similar disagreements in the future.

13. We find something to laugh about.

14. We tell each other that we love each other during the argument. Think about how disarming the tension can be if you start by saying, "I really love you, but ....". Then, think about replacing the word "but" with "and". See how it makes a difference.

15. We tell each other that we love each other again at the end of the argument.

16. We do not keep score. There is no carry over, accumulation of hidden agenda or residual resentment at the end of a disagreement. The brownie point system does not exist in our relationship. This is probably a consequence of rule number 5, more than a standalone rule.

17. We trust each other to respect these rules unconditionally.

18. Mutual respect is never up for grabs. It is there.

19. We always know that no matter what the argument is about, at the end of it, we will still be together. There is never ever a threat or thought that the mar-

riage is at risk. We are in it for the long haul and that is an absolute. At the end of this argument, we will still be "we".

20. We confirm that we love each other. (I know this is a repeat, but (I mean ...AND...) it is worth repeating. Plus, it gives me a nice even number of 20!

These rules are never broken. They just never are. That is the deal. That is how our relationship works when we are dealing with conflict. Having laid the ground rules, what happens with the conflict? Well, Laura and I come at things a little differently. Laura would, in some cases, want to take some time to mull things over. She does not have to get things resolved completely immediately. Sometimes she may not even want to get things resolved immediately.

Not me. That is unacceptable to me. If my wife is unhappy, there is no rest until we are done with it. Oh, there are times when I have tried to let things lie for awhile. I appreciate that in some circumstances that may be what Laura needs more. Ultimately though, I have to keep the ball moving until it is done. In my mind, if my wife is unhappy about any circumstance, it is unbearable for me. I cannot leave things like that for long. I have to get us talking, analyzing, not because I need the analysis. Like I said earlier, my natural tendencies are to just rush through or skip the detailed analysis altogether and jump to the chase or the punch line or the finish line or whatever your favorite cliché is and finish it. However, I have to get through the analysis because I know that is the only way Laura is going to be satisfied with the outcome. That's what she needs. That's what we have to do and my desire to get both of us to the finish line as soon as possible (because I can get there really quickly) is very important for me.

That is our balance. I march us through the analysis because Laura needs it more than me. Laura deals with the analysis that gets us to resolution faster than she may otherwise want to because that is what I need. It all works.

Because of all of this, we never have unresolved disputes at the end of the day. They get dealt with as soon as they arise. In our past there have been times when one of us has chosen to not deal with something right away. Holding back or waiting to have an inventory of issues never is a good idea. It makes the argument so much more complicated to figure out when it does happen. It can be hard to keep track of "who's on first". So, I encourage you to deal with issues immediately.

Sometimes our resolution of a conflict may take quite a while at the cost of sleep. That's OK. That's our choice and it works for us. We always seem to be able to survive a little sleep deprivation and in the long haul, it is worth it.

Laura and I also do other things after an argument is long gone and resolved. Sometimes, much later, after the argument is over, one of us will say, "Remember the other day when we had that disagreement, I just want to talk about what happened there and something about how you responded (or how I responded) to that situation." And we talk about our behaviors. At that point, we can candidly and comfortably discuss our behavior without getting wrapped up in the emotion of the argument. We can explain our responses to certain things the other person did or said by explaining what we perceived at the time. Often it is a real light bulb going on when we state it in those terms. "When you said or did this, I was thinking this and I therefore perceived what you said in this way." It is amazing that often arguments can be abbreviated or avoided altogether if we take the time to better understand what the other person perceives. We do not have to agree with the perception. Addressing the perception can completely alter the problem. So, it is definitely worth taking the time to understand these things. Once again, all of this is just further investment into the couple relationship that you have forged. Now it is just a matter of making it better and better.

This is not the only way to resolve disputes. There are many others. I was talking to some friends about this very thing. Each of them is in long term marriages. Combined, we had ninety years of married experience, male and female, in the discussion. Here are some other ways that they have dealt with disputes in their marriages.

One couple parks the argument until later. They take it as far as they can and then just take a time out. Somehow, they have managed to find a way to compartmentalize the argument and isolate it from the rest of their life. They agree to come back to the dispute at a later time. "It's amazing," my friend said. "Life can go on quite normally with the argument unresolved. All of the emotion is also parked with the dispute. When we come back to the issue, it seems to resolve itself very quickly."

Another friend says that sometimes they just cannot resolve a dispute. They just cannot find a common ground and so they just declare a winner. They accept that they will not agree and he or she decides that he or she is going to do whatever he or she wants to anyway. They have obviously established confidence in each other that when this occurs, whoever "declares victory" does not take advantage of that confidence and the choice is never at the expense of the marriage. Whatever the boundaries are, they both know the marriage comes first. In this circumstance, the choice to declare victory does not breach the tolerance, strength or foundation of the marriage.

One last thing on this whole dispute resolution topic. Before you start an argument, have you ever decided not to? It should be a conscious decision that the argument is worth it. Can you jump through some of the rationalization on your own, come to a resolution that meets your wife's needs and that you can live with and then just go with it without ever letting your wife know that you had to go through this. In other words, just suck it up and go with the flow. Try and do this more often and more consciously when you are tempted to launch into an argument. It's the old count to ten, bite your tongue advice. Do it. I have many times in the past. I know Laura has as well and probably many more times than I have done so. It's what we do.

Think about these things in this context. Will I care about this a year from now? Next month? Next week? Tomorrow? Later today? If your answer is "no" to any of these questions, then maybe you should re-think what you are arguing about. If you get down to the last one and the answer is still "no", then suck it up and do what your wife wants you to do and do it with a smile on your face and love in your heart. Don't worry. She has and will do the same thing for you thousands of times in your life. Teeth marks on tongues quickly heal and fade.

Make Your Wife Feel Special

"A man is incomplete until he is married.
After that, he is finished."

-Zsa Zsa Gabor

I said earlier that marriage is a contact sport; so, wear your pads! It is true. It takes a lot of effort to make a marriage work. You take and give a lot of hits along the way. Eventually, if you work at it – practice, practice, practice – you can get pretty good at this whole marriage thing. There will always be room for improvement. That is also true. You are going to blow it a lot. I do.

Like anything – pick your sport – you cannot get better at it unless you practice. Sitting on the bench or in the stands will never make you a better ball player or hockey player or tennis player or... well, you get it. You have got to get in the game.

True for marriage, too. You will never get better at being a married person unless you get yourself in the game. Observing from the sidelines will get you nowhere. And, I don't mean that you have to get married to get good at marriage. Getting married is sort of a first step minimum requirement. I am talking about just cruising through your marriage as an observer. I think a lot of people kind of do this. They do not invest completely into the marriage. They do not throw themselves into the game and, once there, realize there is no one on the bench to relieve them. There is no second string, no relief pitcher or pinch hitter to come in and replace you in your marriage. There is only you and your wife and the game is on!

Since this is the case, why not try and play the game as best as you can? Why not get really good at it? Why not learn as many skills as you can to make yourself the best husband that you can be so that she can be the best wife that she can be so that you both can have the best marriage that you can possibly have? Might as well. You married her!

This whole book is really about trying to help you do just that. The intent is to make you think about how you spend your efforts and maybe give you a couple ideas about how you may improve as a husband. With this chapter I focus on one basic idea – making your wife feel special. That's the goal. To make your wife feel special, you have to actively love her. You have to take action. There is no other way for you to cause your wife to feel special unless you love her. Love her actively. Love her by doing something or a series of things for her that is all about feeding her needs and wants. Make a dream come true for her.

I know this can all sound a little too perfect fairy-tale dream-land for you, but I know this – every time I have tried to make my wife feel special, and succeeded, it has paid off big time for my own happiness and the strength of our marriage. I never worry about whether she will do the same for me some day. I know that she will. She always has. But who's keeping score anyway? Not me. I don't have to. It doesn't help anyway.

The other thing about trying to do something really special for your wife is that you have to invest time into the preparation of whatever you are planning. Even if the effort does not come off perfectly, it doesn't really matter. What your wife will discover is that you have spent time planning this special thing for her. That means that you have been thinking about her and loving her when she wasn't there. You had to. Otherwise, you could not have planned this thing for her. Do you understand what I am getting at? Evidence that you love your wife (and remember, when I say "love" I mean it as an action) even when she is not there feeds your wife's need to be loved and to know that she is loved. The effort counts. It is not the gift; it is the thought that counts. It really does. Knowing that you have been thinking of her and trying to work out something that is really special for your wife is huge in the "investment in the marriage" category.

This is why a gift purchased by your secretary for your wife is completely valueless. If you ever consider doing this, save your money. It is a waste of time. Find another way to show her you love her. And don't pull out that excuse "I was too busy." I don't buy it and neither does your wife. I know you can get very busy. I have experienced that many times. I just do not use it as an excuse to ignore my wife. I have got a tip for you in the next chapter that will forever deal with the risk of getting too busy.

So, don't give your wife a gift if you have to sub-contract the selection and acquisition of it out to someone else. That is about as meaningful as getting a free sample of laundry softener in your mailbox. Who cares? It just represents someone trying to sell me something and I'm not buying it.

Consider the circumstance when you are sick. You have the flu. You feel miserable. I do not have to go into the details. You know the feeling. When you are sick, you just want someone to take care of you. You want your soup and your blankie and your ginger ale and toast with apple sauce. You want a fire in the fireplace and the remote close at hand. You don't want to have to get up to do anything. And, if you are lucky like me, you have a wife who does all of this for you and more just to help you get through this sickness.

When the roles are reversed and your wife has the flu, you do the same thing for her. You cover her up, bring her the latest issue of her favorite magazine, scramble her some eggs. You would do anything for her to help her feel just a little bit better. You don't even think about whether you should or whether you have to. You want to do all of this because you want her to feel better as soon as possible.

Well, here's a thought. Why do you wait until your spouse is sick to spoil her? Why not spoil her just for the fun of it someday when she least expects it? Why not plan and deliver one special day to your wife? Completely spoil her. It can be done, even with little kids.

My friend, your wife has to know that you love her. No point keeping it a secret. That is not helpful. Get it out there for her to see. The more visible your love for your wife is, the better it will be for everyone. You cannot assume that she knows you love her. You know what? She doesn't know. She hopes you do. She wants you to. But, she cannot know you love her unless you tell her. So, tell her. Every day. Tell her through your words and, more importantly, tell her through your actions.

One way to do this, I have found, is to take an entire day and make it special for my wife. It can be a birthday or anniversary or some other special occasion or, even better, it can be random. I have done this many times for my wife over the years and every time it has been great. Some of these days have become some of our best memories and stories.

Here are just a few examples. Living in Alberta, we have one great geographic advantage – the Rocky Mountains. They are just a short drive from our home. We can make a whole day of it by just getting in the car and driving to the mountains. We pack a picnic, grab some of our favorite CD's and hit the road. We have our favorite spots and we are also open to just exploring new places.

Another idea for a special day is Coupon Day. I got this idea from my sister-in-law and her husband. I think it is a great, inexpensive way to have a fun day together. Every city I have ever lived in has a coupon book of discounts and freebies all over the city. The coupons are for discounts on food, movie passes, two-for-one bowling games or a free bucket of balls at a local driving range – all kinds of stuff. There are also a lot of coupons for oil changes and dry cleaning, but that's not particularly fun on a date! Just go out and buy a coupon book or collect them over time from your junk mail or newspaper. Wrap them up in an old shoe box and give it to your wife as she is waking up in the morning. Tell her to pick her favorite coupons. Her choices will define what you are going to do for the day. It would be a blast to see how much fun you can have for how little money.

Another idea is to just hand your wife a road map of your province or state and say, "Pick a direction". Any direction will do. You can do it randomly. Heads we go north, tails we go south. Then just drive to a small town in the selected direction and see what you can find. Leave every choice and decision for the day up to her. Whatever she wants goes. If she wants to garage sale all day that is what you do. If she wants to find a quiet park and read a book in the sunshine that is what you so. If she wants to have a banana chocolate milk shake with greasy fries that is what you do. The only rule is that there are no errands or jobs or work done on this day. This day is all about what she wants to do and has nothing to do with what she needs to do. Needs can wait for another day.

There are many low cost ways to spend a day with your wife, doing exactly what she wants to do. They can be very casual and easy like what I have just described. With these examples, the real gift is the gift of time together. What you do is not as relevant.

Here is one more idea to make your wife feel very special for a day and you do not even have to be there! A treasure hunt. I have done this for my wife. It is so much fun. Once, when I was gone on a business trip, I set up a treasure hunt in our house for my wife. I hid notes all over the house each note giving my wife instructions to the next note. At the end of the treasure hunt was a surprise.

To start the treasure hunt, I mailed my wife a card with the first clue so that she got it in the mail a day or two after I had left for my business trip. The clues were all silly little rhymes that directed her to the next step. *"I like your lips. I like your toes. Look underneath the garden hose."* Six clues later, she found her surprise – a video of one of her favorite movies, a bottle of root beer (also her favorite) and a bag of microwave popcorn. That was it. Easy. Laura enjoyed the treasure hunt and then enjoyed her night watching a great old movie and she knew the whole time I was thinking about her.

You can do this too. You can even expand on it. You could get friends involved. The clues can direct your wife to a friend's house where they serve her a cup of her favorite tea and then they hand her the next clue that takes her to a spa for a massage. Use your imagination. You can make your wife feel special all day even though you cannot be with her. You just have to put a little effort into the preparation. It is your preparation that shows her, even more, that you are caring for her. She will love you for it.

Laura's fortieth birthday was one special day. It was a day that demanded special attention. A milestone birthday can be received by each person differently. It can be exciting. It can be depressing. It can be melancholy or joyful. It can be something that the person wants to share with others or something that is better spent privately or with only family.

In this case, I knew that Laura would have some mixed feelings about turning forty and I wanted her to feel, more than anything that she is loved, she is talented, she is beautiful and she is special. That was the gift that I wanted her to take away from her birthday. Material things were irrelevant unless they helped me create for her a feeling of being completely loved.

I also knew that Laura felt differently about turning forty than she did about turning thirty. I knew she did not want a big birthday party or anything. So, a surprise party was not going to work. I knew she did not want that and that she was really thinking about what it meant to turn forty. No worries. I had a few ideas for her birthday. There would be no party. However, I wanted her to have a very special experience – a day she would never forget. I wanted her to feel fabulous. I wanted her to feel special, spectacular. I wanted her to enjoy this celebration of her life. I also wanted to give her something that would mean more to her than the usual birthday acknowledgements. I knew one of the best things I could give Laura was time together.

Laura is an artist. She had often said that she would like to try working with pastels. For her birthday I gave her a set of artist's pastels and two pads of pastel paper. We drove to a farmer's field west of Calgary. There, in the field I had set up two chairs, a small table with linens, a crystal bowl of grapes and strawberries, fresh pastries, crystal wine glasses and carbonated fruit juice. Laura and I sat in the sun and breeze, sketched the beautiful scenery of the farmer's land and the rolling foothills as they climbed into the beautiful Rocky Mountains to the west. We talked about us, our children, our happiness. We shared our picnic, toasted the day and us and just enjoyed the time together. (By the way, just in case you are wondering if we just blatantly trespassed on the farmer's property, I had pre-arranged with the farmer for permission to be there.)

On that day I wanted to show Laura that I loved her and that I was paying attention to her. She had said for some time that she wanted to try her hand at pastels. I stored that wish away and made it happen for her. I knew that she wanted a quiet time for her fortieth birthday and I respected that with a picnic for two in a farmer's field. There were other things that happened that day that made the whole day special including a beautiful dinner with our children in Banff and a sleep-over at the Banff Springs Hotel. At the end of the day, Laura knew that I was paying attention to her and she knew that she was loved.

You can do this too for your bride. Your actual plans will certainly be different than mine. They should be. Mine are designed with Laura in mind. You have to tune into what your wife wants and make those wishes come true.

I want Laura to feel special. I want her to know that I love her every day. That is what a marriage should be about – to know that someone is investing their energy in loving you every day and you are doing the same thing right back. We all want to feel that way. It would be great if we felt that way every minute of every day, consciously aware that we are loved and that for at least for one person in this world, we are special. I know that doesn't happen. No one walks around feeling like that all the time. However, it is possible to have that confidence in yourself and in your relationship that may be quietly there, in the background, ready to step up and strengthen you at any time during your life when you really need it.

I am not suggesting that my plans for Laura's birthday are what every guy should do. My point is that it is possible. I am suggesting – no, more than that, I am recommending – that you should consider taking one day and make it special for your wife. It is a great way of showing her how important she is to you. Not only can you fill the day with what you know will please her, but you are also showing that during all the planning and arranging and plotting for that day, you have been focused on her. You have spent your energy and your time dedicated to making her happy. That is not a bad thing to demonstrate to your wife.

Start small. Start with creating a special moment. Consider surprising her with an afternoon of play. Really, all of this goes back to my key suggestion made earlier in this book. Are you paying attention to your wife? Are you listening, watching, learning and retaining what is important to her? Do you know what matters to her? Do you know what makes her happy? You should know these things. The next step is to do something about it. Making one day a special day for your wife is just one way of telling her that your purpose is to make her happy.

Don't know what to do or how to do it? That is not a problem. You do not have to know everything. Here are a few ideas about how you can sort it out.

Your focus should be that everything you do is meant to make your wife happy. So, think about what makes her happy. Think of just one thing and do that.

If you can't think of anything (and I would be really surprised if you couldn't come up with one thing), then just ask. If you want to keep it a complete surprise to your wife (trust me, that's always fun) then, ask her friend or her mother. Ask your kids. Ask someone else who knows her. Tell them what you are trying to do and ask for their suggestions.

Alternatively, if you want, just ask your wife. Tell her what you want to do. Tell her that you want to put together one day that is all about her. Tell her you want to do this, but you want to make it really special and ask her what she would like in that one day. Then, make it happen.

One special moment can lead to another and another and another. There is a snowball effect. Caring for each other begins to feed on itself. It can take over your life. Wouldn't that be great? Two people consumed with making each other happy, wanting nothing more than making the other person feel special and loved. Like the slow, steady consistent investment in a retirement fund, over time the compounding benefits kick in and, one special moment at a time, layered within the days and weeks and years of caring for each other, you have built a spectacular life and an extraordinary marriage.

Ten Tips + a Bonus

"My mother said it was simple to keep a man,
you must be a maid in the living room,
a cook in the kitchen
and a whore in the bedroom.
I said I'd hire the other two and take care of the bedroom bit."

-Jerry Hall

OK. If you have made it this far, you have made it through my five cent philosophy for the extraordinary marriage. But, you may be thinking fine for him, but what am I supposed to do with all of that. I need some practical help to make any of this happen. I just don't know what to do. I am not a romantic guy. I am not sure how I am supposed to make our good (or stale, weakening, dissolving, OK, boring) marriage into something that really makes both of us happier than we have been or imagined we could be.

Well, this chapter is an easy one, probably the easiest one to write. I am going to give you a bunch of ideas that you can actually do right now. Some of these I have already touched upon in the previous chapters. Hopefully some of these will ring true for you. I want you to be able to find something you can do. Steal the idea straight out and do it or modify it, make it fit your wife and do it for her. Make her happy.

Notice I am talking about making your wife happy. This is not about you. In fact, if you have not figured it out yet, I have not been directly concerned about making you, the husband, happy at all. I want you to focus on making your wife happy. If you do that, she will make you happy. You will both be happy and you can build momentum and sustain behaviors beyond that because, quite frankly, everyone likes to be happy and everyone likes to repeat experiences that make them happy.

Not all of these ideas are for everyone. Some may not suit you and your relationship. Some you might just disagree with. That is fine. I am not trying to dictate what must happen for you to improve your marriage. These are just some random ideas that could help you get yourself going in a new direction. It is up to you to figure out the best way to improve your own relationship.

So here are my top ten tips for making your wife happy.

Tip #1 – Dates

Dates are great. They can be anything, as long as they are just for the two of you. Making a decision to date your wife again is one thing. Execution is another. You've got lots of choices as to how to make this happen. Pick the one that will have the best impact on your wife. For instance, you could just simply call your wife and launch into a little role play. Introduce yourself again as the guy she first met. "Hi, this is Jason from third period chem class? I was wondering if you would like to go out with me? To a movie? Tonight?" Play it up. Pretend you are nervous. Maybe you don't have to play that you are nervous. You may actually be nervous. Let her know that. There is nothing wrong with that. Guys have this thing that they have to be in control all the time. What a load of crap.

You could simply tell her that you want some time for just the two of you. Say you want to take her out for dinner, just the two of you, and you do not want to talk about work or kids or the family finances, or the "plan". You just want to talk about anything else. Maybe even come up with a list that is acceptable for the nights' conversation. Send her a written invitation.

I was at a friend's house a few months ago, sitting at their dining room table with several people around the table that I knew, but I really didn't "know", if you know what I mean. On the table was an acrylic box full of cards. On each card there is a question. Each question was designed to spark a conversation. Our friends keep this game on their dining room table and play it with their kids or others when they are visiting. Someone opened up the box and read one of the cards out loud. The whole table instantly became engaged in a conversation that never would have occurred without the cards. Immediately everyone was looking for the next card and we sat there and talked about all kinds of things. That whole experience made the party for me. I got to know these people considerably better than I did before the game and learned more about them in a couple hours than I had known for years. It was great. And the conversations were fun.

It occurred to me then that if any husband and wife are having a little trouble getting on the same wave length and really attending to each other, this is a great game. I suggest you find this game. It is called "Table Topics". Buy it, wrap it up as a gift to your wife. Take your wife out to dinner. At the beginning of dinner, hand her the gift. Let her open it and play the game immediately. Right there in the restaurant.

I guarantee you that you will have conversations you have never had before. And they will not all be heavy, deep emotional conversations. Many will be light and fun. At the end of the night, you will be energized. It is wonderful to have a conversation with your wife that can hold the possibility of surprise. My wife and I have been together over thirty years all together and we still find surprises in the other person. You know why? We are always looking for it, learning more about each other and willing to disclose more things about ourselves all the time. How great is that?

No excuses, my friend. You have to find time for your wife. I think our dating has been good for our children, too. They have grown up witnessing their parents make their husband and wife relationship a priority. Not all of our attention has been invested in raising our children. And you know what? The kids grew up just fine. As it turns out, they didn't need 100% of our attention. They needed a lot of it, but not all. There was plenty of time to be husband and wife, boyfriend and girlfriend, lovers, friends and partners.

Dates can be cheap – a walk to the nearest junk food outlet and then to a park bench. That counts. Time together. That is the thing. Investment in yourselves as a couple, in time that is focused on being a couple, is so important. Mostly what you are trying to do is impress your wife. But for the time being, think of her as your girlfriend. This is the girl you want to get close to. You want this girl to want you, to choose you over all other options. You want her to choose you every day. How can that happen if you are not trying to get to her by providing her with a reason to choose you? Get in the game man!

Tip #2 – Dads Only Baby-Sitting Co-op

You want to go on a date with your bride and you have little kids at home. You need a babysitter. Working out the logistics required to get some time alone with your wife can be challenging. You need to sort that out. Either cough up the cash to pay a babysitter or work it out with family members or get into an exchange agreement with another young family. Two young family dads can work together to both create windows for dating with their respective wives by promising to take on the babysitting responsibilities for the other and tag team the logistical detail. Do you want to speculate how impressed both wives would be if the dads decided to create a dads only babysitting co-op for the sole purpose of facilitating one-on-one dating with your wives? How cool is that? The only way the dads in the co-op will babysit is to allow the other dad to date his wife. No other purpose. This is not to accommodate going to a hockey game, drinking with some old buddies, work. Nothing else. The dads-only-babysitting-co-op-exclusively-for-dating-your-wife. I am telling you that is a winner. Think about it. Do it!

Tip #3 – Surprises

Laura loves surprises. Some people claim they do not like surprises and they throw out warnings like "Don't you ever surprise me. I don't like it."

Nonsense, I say. Everyone likes surprises of some kind. That's like saying you don't like Christmas presents because you don't know what's inside the wrapper until you open it. Of course you like it. Who doesn't like getting a present?

It's how you execute the surprise that may determine if it is received well or not. Some people are really uncomfortable with attention. They just don't like the spotlight focused on them. Surprises in a public environment would not be the best choice for these people. You have to pick your method of execution well.

A surprise date is wonderful if you can handle all of the logistics and simply give your wife a step by step lead into the date. I have already talked about dating, so I will not go into it again and it is just one example. Little gifts of time or service or pampering or just a piece of her favorite dessert from her favorite restaurant all tell her that you are thinking about her and loving her.

The best surprises come when you least expect it and when it is incredibly thoughtful and it demonstrates that you are really paying attention to your wife's needs and wants. When considering this, I encourage you to think beyond the material stuff of life. Don't think about the need for a new electric frying pan because the no-stick surface of the one you received as a wedding gift is still in use fifteen years later and it is worn down to the bare metal. You have to think about what your wife really needs or wants emotionally. That is the highest priority. Working with a junky frying pan a little while longer is not a problem if the emotional needs are met. Now, it may be that the new frying pan would also address the emotional need as well. It all depends on the situation. Ultimately, this all keeps coming back to paying attention and acting.

In my mind, when I consider what will make my wife happy, there really is no difference between "need" and "want". In our life, we are very fortunate. We have been blessed with a wonderful life. From a material perspective, we want for nothing. Of course there is a lot of stuff we don't have that would be considered almost standard equipment in a Canadian middle class home. But that's not because we could not acquire such trappings. It is because we choose not to. We choose – have chosen – differently. So, when I think of a surprise for my wife, I try to address a different sort of thing. I am trying to think of something that would just give her an extra shot of happiness, let her know that especially today, I love her. If the surprise also demonstrates that I have been thinking about her and preparing for the right time to give her this surprise, all the better. I'll explain what I mean by this shortly.

Real surprises are not gifts on her birthday, mother's day, your anniversary, Christmas, Valentine's Day or any other occasion when you would ordinarily give your wife a gift (unless you normally do not give her gifts on these days, and if you don't, why not?) Surprises are random, not predictable, show up out of nowhere. That's why they are surprises. They can be anything – even a new frying pan that shows up magically in the cupboard on a Tuesday morning – if that is something that would really make your wife happy. Why Tuesday? Because it's Tuesday! Do you need a reason or an occasion? Why not Tuesday? It's better than Wednesday, only because it is one day sooner and that means you have taken a step to make your wife happier sooner.

The best kind of surprises are those that speak to your wife's "he loves me" trigger. You have to figure that out. If you don't know what it is, start paying attention and figure it out. Ask her if you have to, but it is really important to know what makes your wife feel loved and love her that way – not exclusively that way – but the more you hit that "he loves me" button, the more she is going to want to respond similarly. It's a great dynamic in your relationship when each of you try to hit homeruns out of the other's "love park". What a terrible analogy, but you get what I mean.

Does your wife love receiving gifts? Does she like it when you vacuum the living room or do the ironing? Does she get excited when you spend time with each other because it happens all too rarely? What is it that she really likes? Whatever it is, do it and do it now. And, from now on, do it randomly.

Surprises can be very small. They do not have to be events. They do not have to be costly. But they can be very, very meaningful as an investment in your relationship. Every prudent investment advisor will always tell you the best way to financial independence and security is to consistently and reliably invest in yourself through regular deposits into your savings or retirement account. Invest your money wisely, steadily over a long period of time. Anyone relying on that big lottery win for your financial security is the fool. What are the odds of that coming through for you?

Well, you don't even have to strain the analogy to make that apply equally to your relationship with your spouse. Think about it. You are not going to hit the mother load with one big single effort at making your wife happy. You may make her happy for a day, but that will not sustain the relationship in the long haul. If you do nothing else to sustain that active loving of your wife, that one day will just stick out as an anomaly in a life of not tending the relationship. In fact, that one day could turn into a real sore spot over time. You can't hang your hat on one day of paying attention to your wife. One hit wonders are soon forgotten.

So, here are some ideas for surprises for your wife.
- Breakfast in bed
- Prepare her a candle-lit bath with quiet music and leave her alone
- Send her to a spa for a massage
- Take her on a picnic

- Flowers (always a favorite)
- Do the ironing
- Clean the kitchen
- Fix the leaky faucet
- Send her off for a day with a friend and hold the fort down at home on your own
- A new dress
- A new pair of slippers
- Write her a love letter and mail it to her
- Give her a card for no reason whatsoever. Tell her you love her and why. Hide the card in her underwear drawer, gym bag or briefcase and just let her find it in her own time.
- Take her on a weekend get-a-way
- Buy or rent a copy of her favorite romantic movie, farm the kids out to neighbors, make some popcorn, open a bottle of wine and watch the movie together.

I could go on and on and on. The possibilities are endless. You have to set yourself up to succeed with this as well. Just don't pull one of these ideas off the list, do it and then sit back and expect tremendous results. Don't expect overnight changes in your relationship with your wife because you did something nice for her. It's that compound interest scenario again. Constant investment in the relationship without any major withdrawals and the compound effect of your investment will make you a wealthy man in the marriage relationship portfolio.

Others will look at you and say, "How did you get so lucky to have a relationship like that?" The answer is that there is no luck involved at all. It's work. It's dedication. It's long term investment. It's paying attention and acting day after day, year after year. It's never neglecting the one human relationship that should matter the most to you in this life.

TIP #4 – Cards

The best thing about giving your wife a card is that it is very portable, it can be delivered in many ways, it is easy and it can be random. Most significantly, if done well, it tells your wife that you are thinking about her and how much she means to you on an ongoing basis. It is not restricted to the "duty" days of recognition like birthdays and anniversaries.

I keep an inventory of cards in a box in my closet. I randomly buy cards whenever I have an opportunity. There are cards I bought for Laura over ten years ago that I still haven't given to her. I just keep them, knowing someday the right circumstance will arise and I will give her the card. I only buy blank cards. I like writing my own note inside. I know not everyone is a Shakespeare. Coming up with something in your own words can be difficult. I know. I understand. But, it is not impossible. In fact, the more difficult it is for you to do, the greater the positive impact it will be on your wife. Think about it. If she knows you have purposely and consciously gone outside your comfort zone just to try and tell her in a unique way that you love her and appreciate her, she will appreciate the effort all the more.

Whatever you write in the card doesn't have to be profound and worthy of immortal preservation in the literature libraries of time. It can be the simplest thing.

> "I watched you brushing your hair this morning, getting ready for another busy day and realized how lucky I am to share my life with this beautiful woman. Thank you."

Or...

"I love your pancakes. Thanks, love."

Or...

"I hate shopping for shoes with you... but I love being with you more. So, let's go shopping."

How easy is that? Simply comment on the smallest of real events that happened today – she makes the best chili in the world, the way she irons sharp creases in your pants, how the towels are folded all perfectly and neatly piled in the linen closet, the sound of her business voice on her office voice mail is sexy, how great her legs look in heels, anything, something personal and real – a small detail of why she is special.

Now there is nothing wrong with the classic "roses are red, violets are blue" Hallmark card verse. If all else fails, let someone else do the writing for you. However, making it personal means so much more. Something in your own handwriting, even awkward and uncomfortable, is probably more meaningful to her than the factory poetry that comes from mass produced greeting cards. Whatever your comfort zone is, just do it. Let your wife know you care.

This stuff is easy. It is no excuse to say, "That's not me." Well, make it "you". Do it. Let her know she is special, she is loved and she is appreciated. Let her know that you are paying attention. Even if you know that she has a dream to paint watercolor flowers, but there is no way your life would accommodate that at this time for any number of reasons, by letting her know that you know she has this dream and it is therefore your dream and your project to make this happen for her someday shows her that you are caring about her dreams. Then, someday make it happen for her. Imagine the importance of her knowing that you know and that achieving her dream is one of your priorities.

All of this can be accomplished in cards, randomly delivered with short notes that say I am paying attention, I am noticing you and I am working on your happiness. This is big.

I have several more ideas about cards and how to use them that I am not going to share with you here. Hey, I want you to use your imagination a little bit. Besides, I have to save some ideas just for Laura. You can work on putting your own original spin on these ideas.

Tip #5 – Gifts

Some women like gifts. Not everyone does. Some women are uncomfortable with receiving gifts. So I am told. I have never encountered someone like that, but I am told they exist. I am going to assume your wife, like mine, enjoys receiving gifts. I am convinced the cost of a gift has nothing to do with the positive impact it can have on the recipient and therefore the relationship.

The impact of a gift is the thoughtfulness of it. The thoughtfulness is reflected in a number of ways. Timeliness, evidence that you are paying attention and presentation are just a few.

Timeliness. I never miss the usual occasions for a gift. I do not care how modest the gift is or needs to be for the sake of family finances, the smallest token will say I respect that we cannot spend money on gifts for each other, but I cannot ignore the occasion or the opportunity to say I love you. So, here is your favorite chocolate bar and a poem (by the way, the poem can be completely silly). I just had to tell you

I love you and thank you for understanding and supporting our bigger need to be thrifty right now.

Timeliness is more than that, though. I keep an inventory of gifts hidden away for Laura. The gifts in my inventory are purchased whenever I come upon them with no specific requirement for gift giving on the horizon. I buy things when I travel. For example, when I go for a haircut, if I walk by a store window and see something that I think Laura would like, I just buy it. I buy stuff all the time and just store it with the others in the closet. I also keep an inventory of gift wrap for all kinds of occasions. Then, when a circumstance arises when I realize NOW would be the perfect time for Laura to receive this gift that I bought a year ago, I go to my inventory, wrap the gift, pull a suitable card out of my card inventory and give it to her. This doesn't happen often. But, it does happen. When it does, when I hit it right, it can make a big difference.

I don't want to make my wife sound like her happiness can be bought with random gifts. That is not it at all. This is just one way that I try to demonstrate to Laura that she is my priority. Her happiness matters. Small things that show her that I am here for her, to be her partner and be with her no matter what she is going through is so very important. There are countless ways to show this. You have to find the ways that can most help your wife feel this.

By many ways, I do mean many ways. There are countless ways. You have to find as many ways as possible to constantly communicate this to your wife.

Gifts that hit the mark, that show your wife that you are paying attention are very important. If your wife wants to paint, giving her a new X-box is not going to cut it. If she loves her garden, tickets to the Monster Truck Rally next Sunday kind of misses the mark. If she would love more time with you, just to be a couple, a weekend in Vegas with the in-laws just confirms with her that you just don't get her.

So, what does your wife really want? If she wants to paint, buy her a French easel, canvas boards, some acrylic paints and brushes. Set the easel up in the corner of the guest room, blindfold her and guide her to the room and then remove the blindfold. Sign her up for painting lessons at the local arts college. Take the course with her. Create the space in your life for her to enjoy this. Let it feed her heart. Take the kids away from that space for her. Protect it for her. Let her enjoy this for herself (or together with you if you choose to take the class with her) and let that desire be satiated for her. That shows you are paying attention.

Gifts can be many things, not just stuff in a box. Gifts can be time. Time alone, so she can enjoy the quiet and rest her mind. Time with you, so that you can be boyfriend and girl-friend again. Time with friends, so that she can be with other adults, enjoying adult things, rather than buried in the sticky, peanut butter and jam world of toddlers every waking mo-ment of her life.

A perfect gift can be something as simple as the newest edi-tion of her favorite magazine or the newest book by her fa-vorite author, a glass of wine, a fire in the fireplace, a new CD. Anything that speaks to something she really loves. Spoil her – if only long enough for her to open the gift, realize that you care and then you are all off again into the chaos of kids' sports and family commitments. At least in the chaos, she knows you have been thinking about her and paying attention.

Tip #6 – No Television

No television in the bedroom. We never fell into this trap. And, I do mean trap. That is what it is. You put a television in your bedroom and you are just taking away from the opportunity to create an environment for just the two of you. Take it out. When you are in your bedroom, it is your sanctuary. I think it is a mistake to get used to having the television handy when you go to bed. It becomes a habit to click it on, zone out with the evening news or late night talk shows and forget about the person lying beside you. I owe this tip (and many others) to my wife. Early in our marriage we had an experience with a television in our room and Laura pointed out how quickly I became hooked on turning the TV on as soon as I walked in the room. Our pattern of intimacy changed instantly and I became less attentive to my wife. Thankfully, she called me on it and right away we recognized that having the TV in our bedroom would be destructive to our marriage. It is the one room in our home that is really reserved just for us. In an earlier chapter I said the bedroom is reserved for us and the kids are not invited. Well, the TV is just like another kid – relentless. It will demand and take all your attention if you let it. Don't let it.

Laura and I were on a cruise celebrating our twenty-fifth wedding anniversary and got involved with an on board "Newlywed Game". If you are at least as old as me, you will recall the old television show where four newlywed couples would compete by answering a number of questions about each other in the absence of their spouses and then the spouses were returned to the studio to answer the same questions. If their answers matched those of their spouse, they were awarded points. The couple with the most points at the end of the game won a prize – usually something for their home like a washer and dryer or new fridge.

Anyway, on the ship, Laura and I were picked to be one of the couples on the cruise version of the game. The four wives were shuffled off into another room while the husbands were asked four questions. One of the questions asked of us was "When you wake up in the morning, what is the first thing you reach for?" One of the other couples playing the game was a newlywed couple who had been married for just five days. His answer to the question was "Uh... the remote?" The room moaned when he said that. However, when his new bride returned and was asked the same question, she said, "the remote." The room exploded with laughter. The remote! Are you kidding me? They had only been married for five days. If that really was the first thing he went for when he woke up, what hope is there for their future? That television is going to ruin the best opportunity to build an intimate relationship with each other.

So, take the TV out of your bedroom. That room is all about the two of you. Take advantage of it. Do not dilute it with distractions.

Tip #7 – Protect Your Space

Keeping the bedroom for just the two of you directly relates to my next tip. I believe your bedroom should be reserved for just you and your bride. No one else is invited. When you have a new baby, it is convenient and practical to have the new baby close by if mom is nursing. I also understand the times when children have their nightmares and get scared and come into your bedroom and ask if they can sleep with mom and dad. Those situations occur all the time. It is my belief that these should be kept to a minimum. I strongly encourage you to establish early and immediately with your children that Mom and Dad's bedroom belongs to Mom and Dad. It is not a family room. Mom and Dad's bed is not a family bed. I encourage you to move the baby into his or her own room as soon as possible. I encourage you to not share your bed with your children but for the most exceptional circumstances.

I believe that a couple needs their space to be husband and wife to each other. Children need to know this. Your bedroom is where you can be husband and wife, not Mom and Dad. It is important. Create a place for just the two of you in your home. Your kids will understand and accept it and your marriage will be better for it.

A lock for your door works, too!

Tip #8 – Take Care of Yourself

Who wants a husband who does not have enough respect for himself to take care of himself? Keep yourself clean and groomed. If your belly is beginning to hide your belt buckle under a fold of flab, eat a salad, take a walk, pass on the Doritos and beer and do something about yourself. It is not a big deal to show a little self discipline. You should want to be the very best person you can be for yourself and your wife. You owe it to yourself and to her to take care of yourself. Take your health seriously.

I am not saying that if you don't have six pack abs that you are a failure as a husband. If that is the measure, we are all in trouble. But, you promised on your wedding day to be there for your wife for your entire life. A part of fulfilling that promise is to make sure you are doing what you can to keep yourself healthy so that you can support her and be strong for her for so long as she needs you.

If you are not taking care of yourself, if you are evolving into that lovely pear-shaped body that so many men acquire as they sloth into middle age, then, stop it. Do something about it. In fact, you can take this as an opportunity to create an activity that you and your wife can share together. Why don't you start exercising regularly? Take a walk around the neighborhood. Better yet, invite your wife to take that walk with you. During the walk talk about your fitness. Discuss how together you may develop a plan to focus a little more on your health. Suggest taking regular walks together as a start. Start making better decisions about your eating. It doesn't take much to turn a sedentary lifestyle into an active lifestyle. Give it a go. You have a responsibility to take care of yourself.

TIP #9 – No Porn

When staying in a hotel, the first thing I do as soon as I get into my room is grab the remote. I turn on the television. Then I open the in-room movie menu and immediately hit the buttons to block the adult movie titles from the television. I do not even stop to think about it. I just do it as soon as I get in the room. It takes less than ten seconds and those adult movies are blocked. Then, if I am ever tempted to watch that kind of stuff, I have to contact the front desk and ask that the adult titles be re-installed in my room. I will never make that call. I bet 99.99% of all men would never make that call.

Internet porn is also easily available. Who is to stop you in the privacy of your hotel room? It is only you. Knowing what is right does not always translate to good decisions. We are all human. At times we are all weak. We are all imperfect.

Hey, pornography is tempting. I have certainly been tempted by it. When I first started travelling with my work, I was amazed by the accessibility to pornography in my hotel room. They made it easy for me. I did not have to admit to anything.

Movie titles never showed up on the hotel bills. I could, in the privacy of my hotel room, watch explicit sex all alone. No one would ever be hurt. No one would ever know. Why not? Same thing with internet porn. No one would ever know.

I tried it. I was curious. I thought, hey, I am an adult. There is nothing illegal about this. I am not hurting anyone. I am entitled to this. It's a free country. I can do this and it is OK.

Well, I have to tell you, it is not OK. I did not handle it very well. I could not sit through the movie. After just a few minutes I had to turn it off. I had to stop. I felt dirty, deceitful and dishonest.

I also try to protect myself against the temptation of internet porn. You know what? The software programs you can install on your home computers to keep your kids away from inappropriate websites work on laptops in hotel rooms, too. That's what I do. You know why? Because I am imperfect. I am just an ordinary guy. I am capable of making bad choices even when I don't want to. So, I try to minimize the risk.

The bottom line is that we husbands promise to honor our wives all the days of our lives. That is a part of that wedding day promise. The biggest challenge in honoring our marriage is to do it when no one is looking. That is when we have to stand up for ourselves, our wives and our marriages and remind ourselves of our commitment.

I promised. I said, "I will honor you *all* the days of my life", not just the days when my wife is physically with me. To do this, I must always try to conduct myself in an honorable way. One way I try to do this is by blocking pornography out of my hotel television and my laptop.

Tip #10 – Hugs

My wife and I were having dinner and I asked her to give me some more ideas about tips. The first thing out of her mouth was, "hugs". Hugs, she said, are, in many circumstances, way better than words. They speak a different language and actually have a much larger vocabulary than the verses written by the great poets. I know it works for us. Touching each other affectionately, often, regularly, is one of the primary ways we let each other know that we are thinking of each other, that we love each other. Laura and I barely ever walk by each other without some loving touch. Sometimes, I admit, I sneak in a "naughty" touch. Actually, I do that a lot. Now don't be looking for it if you are with us in a social setting. Over the years, I have become expert at this. Some touches are fleeting. So brief and light, but there is an awareness of each other that we constantly share. It communicates all sorts of things all the time. We love it.

I know not everybody likes to be touched, especially in public. Some people are uncomfortable with physical contact, particularly those who may be victims of sexual or physical abuse. I understand that. This tip (as with all of them) is not intended for everybody. But, consider it. I always find it amazing when couples are together in a social setting – a cocktail or dinner party – and, other than arriving together, they barely spend any time together the entire evening. You wouldn't even know they were together unless you knew them or saw them arrive or depart together.

When Laura and I are at a party, you know we are together. We are not joined at the hip or anything. We enjoy socializing with others and often go our separate ways as the natural flow of socialization and conversation carries us around the party. But, we are always aware of each other. We seek each other out. A glance across the room. We have secret signals that can communicate a myriad of things to each other without ever speaking a word and are understood from across a crowded room and we also regularly connect with each other and spend time together as a part of our socializing.

When I was growing up, my parents and their generation of our family have a bizarre routine of men in the basement watching sports or playing cards and the women in the kitchen. That's it. If you are male, you are in the basement. If you are female, you are not. When Laura and I were dating, she joined me for an extended family gathering at my parents house – probably Christmas or Easter dinner. I was playing my role as the up-and-coming he-male of the pride. I was nestled into a seat on the couch in the basement, happily taking in the conversation of my father and his friends (my uncles) as they pontificated on the issues of the day. Usually this circled around the price of grain and health of the crops, the performance of the local sports teams or other farming news and gossip. Hockey and baseball were always hot topics and my uncle Jim often liked to trash the politicians of the day.

Quite to everyone's shock, Laura, my beautiful girlfriend, descended the basement stairs and sat beside me on the couch. I looked at her, a little embarrassed. She was interfering in the well established behaviors of this particular herd. She was imposing her femaleness on the males in the testosterone arena of the clan.

"What are you doing here?" I asked. "You are supposed to be up with the women."

"What am I supposed to do up there?" she asked. "I don't know anyone up there? I came here to be with you."

Right there a light went on and I saw the behavior of my family, well established over the generations, as odd. Why do we separate like that? It seemed so odd to me. I agreed with Laura and we both left the man den and moved up stairs together. I have to say that it felt a little odd to do so. I felt I had to respect the traditions of the family. So, I chose to be with her and take the step to enter the female sanctum with her. That, I thought was an easier adaptation. At least I knew everybody in both pools.

I have noticed that my family somehow grew out of that ritual over the years. Maybe it was the influence of the next generation. However, I bet there are still a lot of people who tend to fall into the pattern of separation from your spouse when in a larger social setting. That is my point.

Laura and I stay connected. Even in a social setting with others, we stay physically connected. That physical connection often leads to more interesting and enjoyable physical entanglements later in the evening when we are alone because all night, even in a crowd, we are communicating with each other that the other person is on our mind.

BONUS TIP – One Bottle a Day

No, I am not talking about twelve ounces of single malt scotch for you!

I wanted to end this chapter with ten tips. I have got a long list of them. However, I want to share one more tip with you because I think it is critically practical to sustaining your life together as a couple. I talk a lot about spending time as a couple and making the marriage a priority. This bonus tip is a very practical suggestion to help accomplish that.

For young fathers or men who are about to become fathers for the first time, this is one of the most important tips I can offer you and it is incredibly practical because it opens up so many opportunities for you. This tip facilitates your ability to maintain a couple-ness about your relationship with your wife while surviving the chaos and adjustment of a new member of the family imposing himself or herself (or themselves) onto your forever lost "couple only" life.

When you have children, talk to your wife about feeding the children. If your wife wants to breast feed, that is great. I think there are many studies and evidence that show babies who are breast fed benefit in a myriad of ways. These benefits are not just physical health (reduction in risk of allergies, for example) but also the nurturing and bond that is created and strengthened with mom every time she feeds her baby. So, I am all for breast feeding. I also know that not all babies breast feed well. In our family we batted five hundred on the breast feeding. Our boys took to it like crazy, but the girls (twins) did not breast feed and ultimately we fed them with bottles. That turned out to be a great thing, really, because of how Laura and I were able to share the load of feeding and changing the twins. Needless to say, with two more children three-and-under in the house, managing new-born twins was a busy time.

Anyway, the tip for young fathers is this. Always make sure your new baby takes one feeding a day from a bottle. Mom can pump her milk (that's what Laura did) or you can use formula. It's your decision and I am not advocating one over the other. What I am advocating is the practice of always feeding the baby with a bottle once a day.

This does three things. First, it gives Mom a break. When the baby is not sleeping through the night and needs to be fed, Dad can step in, feed the baby with the bottle, change him / her/ them and settle the baby back down. Mom gets a chance to sleep through the night for once. Those of us who have been through this know the importance of giving Mom an occasional reprieve at this exhausting stage of parenthood. These early weeks and months with a new baby can be very hard on everyone's sleep. Your wife needs rest. One bottle a day enables you to give her that rest.

The bottle feeding can also be at another time in the day that allows your wife to nap, take a bath or get some quiet. Whatever. Use the bottle to create an opportunity for your wife to have whatever she needs for herself. She deserves it.

The second benefit of one bottle a day is that Dad gets an opportunity to have that special time with baby. Trust me, it is special. Take advantage of it. In fact, you deserve it. You are entitled to it and should try to find a way to have some close, intimate time when the baby is sleeping, feeding or pooping and you get to clean it all up. This helps you build your relationship with your baby as well. It's great.

The third reason – and this is the big payoff – is that a babysitter can feed the baby. It does not have to be you or your wife. One bottle a day creates a window of opportunity for you and your wife to get out, get away from baby and change tables and burping blankets and be a couple. It gives you time to continue to court your wife as a "girlfriend" (something I have spent a fair bit of time about early in this book). Without the bottle, you are locked onto a schedule. Baby's schedule does not create a lot of time to be a couple. You have to create it. You have to make it work. You have to always continue to find a part of your life for just the two of you.

One bottle a day facilitates your life long courtship of your bride. You must do this. Life as father and provider can overtake life as husband, boyfriend and lover. These roles are all important, but father should not trump lover and husband. They have to co-exist. It is my belief that you are a better father if you are first a great husband. You have the gift of being both. Do not let one role atrophy from lack of attention.

Your father role will last your lifetime, but, the time dedicated to fulfilling that role will, just by passage of time, diminish. Husband and lover will dominate your life's role again. You need it to be healthy and strong and vigorous for the long haul.

So, those are some tips. I could go on and on and on. There are literally hundreds, maybe thousands, of ideas that can be shared and considered. Not all of them are for everybody. I know that. Simple, every day opportunities accumulate. Remember the compound interest example. That's what this is really about. So, invest every day. Keep investing. Tell your wife she is beautiful. Show her she is. Compliment her on something she is doing or has done for you or for herself. Support her interests. Create and protect time to be together as a couple. Touch her and tell her you love her. Surprise her with love notes or small gifts that you know are meaningful for her. Give her the day off and take care of everything in the house for her for one day.

You need to discover what matters to your wife. What makes her feel appreciated, loved, beautiful, wanted, sexy, desirable? If you do not know, ask her. If you do know, do something about it. Feed her wants and dreams. You will win big time in the end.

We Are the Examples

The challenge is there for every husband. We married men have a great duty and obligation. It is the duty to build the strongest marriages we can notwithstanding our human imperfection. It is in spite of our humanity that this noble goal must be pursued and it is because of our humanity that we need it. We are going to make so many mistakes along the way that they will be impossible to count. We should not be counting anyway. By building our marriages and working on them every day we have the opportunity to not only make our wives happy, we have the opportunity to become better individuals and ultimately find a wonder-filled happiness for ourselves.

We also have the opportunity to witness to the world that this relationship and covenant that is marriage is a wonderful vocation. We are the examples. Our children are watching. Our friends are watching. Our children's friends are watching. By our lives we are declaring what we believe to be right. By our daily choices we are telling the world what is important to us and we are acting out the instruction manual for pursuit of happiness and love in this life.

The gift of marriage is a choice. We have the option to choose it or not, but if we choose it, we accept the responsibility TO LOVE AND HONOR our wives every moment. This is borne out in our every action, our every choice. It is not a silent state of mind or feeling. It is action.

I challenge you to pick up this task of being a walking daily example of true marriage. Display for all to see how wonderful and fulfilling it is. I said earlier in these pages that it is a battle. Well it is, not just personally for each of us in our own marriages, but also for those who are watching. We stand as our example of the beautiful relationship of a man and women joining their lives into one, giving unselfishly to each other until death we do part and we are doing this in opposition to a society that does not value marriage. We are battling against the overwhelming societal influences of convenience.

Our children are bombarded with every social infusion and influence that says marriage is not important. It is unnecessary, disposable, and casual. We must be relentless in our commitment of fulfilling our vows and stand as examples of the joy of marriage. How better to do this than to live a life that is a testament to this joy and love and all that flows from it?

Our opportunity as husbands is bigger than our respective marriages – it is our example to the world, to the next generation who are bombarded with contrarian evidence – much of which our generation has created – that marriage is not worth it. We have an obligation to provide a living example of what marriage is intended to be. What it can be. We take that on as much as we take on the lifelong commitment to never stop working on building our own marriages into the best source of love and kindness and passion and compassion and giving that we can. Our love given in our marriage will pour out for all to see, to witness, to swim in, to drink up and possibly to take on, build upon it for themselves until it is spilling over and out from them. This is what we can do. This is what my God is calling me to do. This is the best thing I can do with my life. The rest flows from this.

All other accomplishments pale in comparison to a loving marriage shared by two imperfect people who pursue that one relationship, undaunted by the bumps and bruises suffered along the way, for their entire lives. By doing that, everything else becomes possible.

"I promise to love you and honor you all the days of my life."

Remember... IT'S A VERB!

Let's hear from you!

"All marriages are happy. It's the living together afterward that causes all the trouble."

-Raymond Hull

Tell me what you think. Get back to me. Drop me a line. Go to www.ordinary-guy.com and complete the survey, participate in the online discussion forums or just send me a note. I am trying to gather as much input from people just like you so I can do a better job of helping others discover and enjoy the best that a wonder-filled marriage can offer. That's all I care about. Send your thoughts and ideas to me. Send them anonymously if that helps. I only ask that you be honest. What works for you? What doesn't work for you? Stories and anecdotes – good and bad – all help build a body of information and experiences that I will try to use to improve marriages.

If you would like me to come and speak to your church group, community, social club or organization, I would love to do that. Drop me a line. Let's see what we can work out.

Time for a Quiz!

You can find Ordinary Guy Extraordinary Marriage on the internet. Our website is:

www.ordinary-guy.com

The questions below are a part of a survey that can be found on the website. It would be great if you logged on and answered the survey on line. That way we can build an inventory of more input from as many people as possible who have experience with the whole marriage relationship. Over time, we hope to build a body of information and ideas that can be used in further publications and articles on our website.

The purpose of all of this is simple – to build stronger, more fulfilling and happier marriages.

So please consider completing the survey on line. If not, just answering the following questions honestly and having your wife answer the questions as well and then sharing your answers with each other may spark a very constructive and enlightening conversation and may help you learn a little more about each other that can give each of you an opportunity to love the other one more. That, all by itself, is good enough reason to take the time and do the survey.

1. Why did you marry your wife/husband?
2. Why did he/she marry you?

3. What is your favorite thing about your wife/husband?

4. Does he/she know that?

5. What is her/his favorite thing about you?

6. How do you know?

7. What is it about your wife/husband that you don't get?

8. What is it about you that your wife/husband doesn't get and you wish she/he did?

9. What is the number one behavior/experience you would like to change in your marriage?

10. What surprised you about marriage in a good way?

11. What surprised you about marriage that you have not been able to reconcile?

12. What has caused the greatest conflict in your marriage?

13. How did you resolve it?

14. What has given you the greatest joy in your marriage?

15. How have you nurtured it?

16. What is the most important thing you need from your spouse?

17. Are you getting it? Yes? Why? No? Why not? What are you doing about it?

18. What is the most important thing he/she needs from you?

19. Is he/she getting it? Yes? Why? No? Why not? What are you doing about it?

20. Have you told/showed your wife/husband that you love her/him today?

About the Author

Terry Bachynski was born in Woodslee, Ontario in 1957. After graduating from the University of Western Ontario with an LL.B. in 1981, he moved to Calgary, Alberta. Terry's career in the resource development business resulted in the family moving back and forth between Calgary and Fort McMurray and ultimately found them living in Edmonton, Alberta.

Terry and his wife, Laura, were married in 1982. They enjoy many interests together and are active in their faith community. Their children are all busy chasing their own dreams in various post secondary educational institutions around North America.

Ordinary Guy – Extraordinary Marriage is Terry's first book for public consumption, although he has a few other efforts under his belt that were written for just his wife.

Husbands, love your wives, just as Christ loved the church and gave himself up for her to make her holy, cleansing her by the washing with water through the word, and to present her to himself as a radiant church, without stain or wrinkle or any other blemish, but holy and blameless. In this same way, husbands ought to love their wives as their own bodies. He who loves his wife loves himself. After all, no one ever hated his own body, but he feeds and cares for it, just as Christ does the church— for we are members of his body. For this reason a man will leave his father and mother and be united to his wife, and the two will become one flesh.

Ephesians 5: 25-31